# Island Farm

# Island Farm

**Arthur Versluis**

Michigan State University Press
East Lansing

Michigan State University Press
East Lansing, Michigan 48823-5202
Printed and bound in the United States of America.

04  03  02  01  00    1  2  3  4  5

LIBRARY OF CONGRESS CATALOGING-IN-PUBLICATION DATA

Versluis, Arthur, 1959-
Island farm / Arthur Versluis.
p. cm.
ISBN 0-87013-545-7 (pbk. : alk. paper)
1. Farm life—Michigan—Grand Rapids—Anecdotes.
2. Family farms—Michigan—Grand Rapids—Anecdotes.
3. Versluis, Arthur, 1959-
I. Title.
S521.5.M5 V47 2000
630.'9774'56—dc21

99-050563


Cover and Book design by Michael J. Brooks


Cover artwork is "Spring in the Valley" and
is used by permission of the artist, Jeremy
Holton (www.jeremyholton.com).


Visit Michigan State University Press on the World Wide Web at:
www.msu.edu/unit/msupress

# CONTENTS

The glory of the farmer is that, in the division of labors, it is his part to create. Men do not like hard work, but every man has an exceptional respect for tillage, and a feeling that this is the original calling of his race, that he himself is only excused from it by some circumstance which made him delegate it for a time to other hands. And the profession has in all eyes its ancient charm, as standing nearest to God, the first cause.

The farmer is permanent, clings to his land as the rocks do. In the town where I live, farms remain in the same families for seven and eight generations. . . He who digs a well, constructs a stone fountain, plants a grove of trees by the roadside, plants an orchard, builds a durable house, reclaims a swamp, or so much as puts a stone seat by the wayside, makes the land so far lovely and desirable, makes a fortune which he cannot carry away with him, but which is useful to his country long afterwards.

—Ralph Waldo Emerson,
"Farming," in *Society and Solitude* (1870)

The proceeds from the sale of this book will go
toward preserving our family's land.

# Preface

Another Saturday morning at ten in the coffee shop. Around us is the murmur of conversation as people stroll to booths nearby, carrying their breakfast trays or coffee cups, maneuvering among others who are standing up preparing to leave. Those of us who work on our family farm have come to the coffee shop at ten o'clock ever since my cousins and I were children. Years ago, we went to the Delight Grill, where we sat in the dim light on chrome-legged chairs; later, we went to the donut shop owned by a heavyset Italian fellow who had evidently broken his nose long ago in a fight; and later still we went to Mr. Fables, for years, until they closed the restaurant and put the building up for sale. Now we have found another place to settle down on a cold winter morning. The coffee isn't too bad, but that's not why we come here.

I sit down in a booth across from my cousin Peter Joe, who smiles and asks what's been going on with me lately. Peter Joe and I grew up together, as his father's house is just to the south of my family's; my mother taught us both how to multiply and divide, using board games she created for us, and I remember he and I playing Daniel Boone and Davy Crockett among the trees and in the fields. Pete and I share some resemblance to one another, at least in blond hair and worn Levi's jeans, flannel shirts and heavy winter coats. As Pete and I talk, our cousin Nathan sits down, and he joins in the conversation. Nathan, tall and strong, with tousled dark blond hair and a warm smile, works on our family farm with Peter Joe, Pete's dad (my Uncle Dave) and Jim Van Dyken, who's sitting with Nathan's dad, my Uncle Warren, in the next booth over. Jim, a tall fellow with the languid, sure movements of an athlete, has worked on our farm since his days at Calvin College some years ago, and married into my Uncle Warren's family. He and my Uncle Warren are engaged in a conversation during which my Uncle Warren suddenly lets loose a barrel laugh. My Uncle Warren's a rare combination: a poet's sensibility in a man whom his brothers call "Tiny," and who I've seen toss entire bales of hay into a haymow using a pitchfork.

In the meantime, a few more family members have joined us. My father, the eldest of the four brothers, sits down with my Uncle Dave in a booth across the aisle. They both have sunburned faces and thick hands; my Uncle Dave's hair is still yellow-blond and tousled, though he's now near retirement age. They're talking about the lack of concern our local representatives and senators show for the working man, let alone for the farmer. "They don't even know there are farmers in Michigan," my Uncle Dave says, leaning back. "No," my father replies, "all they listen to are corporations, and they're shipping every job out of this country as fast as they can. Maybe pretty soon people will eat information instead of food." In the next booth my Uncle Jim Morren is sitting down, and he nods to us and grins as he sits, moving with the grace of a man who's worked in construction all his life. A natural builder and designer, he built his house himself, and then designed and constructed an outside woodstove with recirculating water to heat the house. His sons, Henry, Bill, and Glen, have all worked on the farm with us, and only last week Henry was in town. "Bill is coming in next weekend," Nathan tells me. "How about Vince?" Pete asks. "Vince who?" Nathan replies with a laugh. Vince is another cousin who works down south now as an archaeologist.

Our Uncle Phil comes in, wearing a jet black Russian winter hat with a small red and gold Communist insignia on the front, the hat's ear pieces hanging down over a thick down coat. Bearded, he looks a little like Walt Whitman. In the farming partnership, he's done the bookkeeping for more than four decades. He and Peter Joe talk farm business for a moment and then he sits down in the booth to the south, across from him my cousin Peter Phil, with dark hair and a moustache, elected a local judge not long ago, and his brother Chad, who's now a commercial realtor. There was a time when the four of us—Pete, Chad, Peter Joe and I—were quite close. All around the same age, we worked on the farm for years. Now, we mostly see each other in the coffee shop on Saturdays, or at the occasional family reunion.

In the booth next to my father and my Uncle Dave is my cousin Dave, and his son Dave, now in high school. My cousin Dave, the one with tousled brown hair and wire-rimmed glasses, an artist and graphic designer, is sitting across from his brother Steve, who teaches high school and is a city commissioner. Steve and I have often talked in the field about literature and history, interests he shares with my Uncle Warren and me. As a teacher, Steve still can help out on the farm during the summer; we work in the strawberry fields each year, as does my father and my Uncle Warren. I help out when I can as well, although my time has been increasingly taken up by work at the university and by research and publication. Now, in winter, Peter Joe, Jim, Nathan, and Uncle Dave spend their time trimming trees, or in some cases, cutting down entire orchards, and we help out only on special occasions, like loading heavy cut limbs onto trailers and hauling them away for firewood.

My Uncle Warren is the family and city historian, and we've spent many a winter hour poring over his collection of maps of our farm's vicinity dating back to 1836. It's from my Uncle Warren and from my dad that I have learned the most about our family's history. Today, he's brought along a copy of the earliest known map of the Grand River Valley, and we look over with interest a topography that's now almost unrecognizable. As we look over the landscape surveyed by Lucius Lyon in 1836, we can see only a mission and a few other notations right along Grand River itself. No city, almost no cabins—only a pattern of abstract squares laid out from the river westwards, a grid that belies the forests and swamps and clearings that must have been there. Even today, in a few places, you can see the remnants of the wilderness, the canopy of oaks that covered the hilly lands above the river valley itself, the slope of the high land where forest and then orchard gave way to subdivisions and strip malls.

As the buzz of conversation surrounds us, we talk about the first settlers in our area, mostly English and Irish farmers, then a few Germans, and only later some Dutch. I have often wondered what this landscape looked like one hundred and fifty years before. Only on our farm and in a few wooded places near the river can one garner some sense of that now distant past, so much has the landscape changed. When my father and uncles and aunts grew up on what was then my grandfather Peter's and granduncle Paul's farm, the major highway to the north of the farm—from whose constant traffic roar one cannot escape now—was but a two-lane road in the rural countryside. Our farm was rural, even fifty years ago, and surrounded by other farms—Malloy, Dykstra, Graham, farming names that now have meaning only in my family's collective memory. By those names, we designate parts of our farm, now the last working farm partially within the actual city limits of Grand Rapids.

To our west, and outside the city limits, is the Engelsma farm, but thirty-five acres of that has just been sold for condominiums by Ted Engelsma, who's now in his seventies and still farming. The Engelsmas have orchards too; in fact, I just saw Jim Engelsma, who's in his mid-thirties, before coming to the coffee shop. Every Saturday in the fall and early winter, he parks his pickup truck on a corner nearby and, accompanied by his little daughter, sells apples, apple cider, and honey. Today, he looked cold in his thick tan jacket and worn gloves, his tan face reddened a little in the cold air, but he was in good spirits as usual. This past year wasn't a good one for apple growers, but he's hopeful that the next year will be better. Every farmer is hopeful, I think. He seemed surprised when I first stopped to buy cider and honey from him, but the way I see it, we're not in competition with one another as much as all in the same boat, adrift on an indifferent and sometimes hostile sea.

As my cousins and I grew up, the suburbs overtook our area, sprawling outward into the fertile black soil along the river far west and south of us. Farm after farm vanished underneath nearly identical suburban lawns and vinyl-sided houses, strip malls and supermarkets, banks and gas stations, apartments and condominiums, churches and more suburbs. The highway grew more and more congested and dangerous as traffic on it increased exponentially. Not far from us, an apartment complex went in atop what had been an orchard, its apartment walls so thin you can hear your upstairs neighbor's conversation on the telephone. Across the highway, more apartments went in atop a cornfield that we had rented for years in order to grow sweet corn for our farm market. People began to ride motorcycles and snowmobiles across our property, running over young apple trees, leaving behind long black skid marks where their vehicles roared and slid through the orchards and fields.

One wing of our family, that represented by my Uncle Phil, his wife Joyce, and their children Peter Phil and Chad, purchased the former Graham farm across the highway, the last hundred acre farm within the city limits of Grand Rapids. It had been a former agricultural experiment station for Michigan State University, and when we were growing up, the sound of the university spray rig howling in the distance, applying one or another experimental pesticide, was as familiar as the sound of geese or blackbirds. For a few years, our family farm rented the orchards and fields from their new owners, and we grew tomatoes and sweet corn, strawberries and pears and apples. It was good soil, well drained and productive. But eventually they sold the back half of the farm for suburban housing, and now the houses stand only a few feet apart, almost identical and in rows, more generic than those of Levittown, all that topsoil having been pushed about by giant earthmovers so as to create walkout basements for house after house after house. I have a photograph of Jim Van Dyken cultivating and fertilizing young sweet corn, leaning aside to watch the passing green plants beneath the small red Farmall tractor, behind him a steep, barren, eroded slope downwards like an artificial canyon, upon which one can see an earthmover the size of a building. It is a strange juxtaposition.

That is the kind of juxtaposition we have to live with, nowadays. My father, having in his lifetime seen so many farms disappear, and so much farmland vanish forever under earthmovers and pavement, is philosophical about its loss. My mother and sisters are less so—they wonder when our society will begin to recognize that we should not destroy all our farmland. We all wonder how any farmers can survive in a society that seems so totally indifferent to the loss of irreplaceable farmland, and to the loss of farming family after farming family who cannot make a living in a world ruled by giant corporations and the legislators they so often purchase. It wasn't too long ago that a politician showed up in the coffee shop and went about shaking hands with everyone. When he reached John Dykstra, a burly retiree coffee shop regular, and introduced himself as a candidate, John recoiled as if he were about to touch a leper's open sores. "Get away!" he said in horror. While I don't want to be as cynical as John about politicians, I have yet to meet a single living politician at any level who genuinely speaks on behalf of the farmer and preserving farmland. Perhaps I don't get out enough.

But you can see how, as I look out over the coffee shop crowd, I can be surprised and grateful that we have made it this long, that we still exist as a functioning family farm while on the edge of a city and surrounded by suburbia. That we do exist is due partially to the family camaraderie, to the fact that we all grew up together working on this high, well-drained, fertile land some thirty miles from Lake Michigan; we share the common aspiration of keeping the land as farmland and the family farm itself alive for future generations. It was 1896 that our great-grandfather purchased the first fifteen acres of the family farm, and despite everything, we remain optimistic that one way or another, the farm will continue. Peter Joe and his wife Sandy, now living with their children in the family's main farmhouse on the hill, have every right to expect to be working the farm decades from now. The time will come, Pete once told me, when the government will pay people just to preserve what little is left in this country of farms and farmland, and I have no doubt that's true. It's the meantime that concerns us.

Eventually, we begin to stand, stretch, and walk out into the cool winter air. I ask Pete where they're working—trimming over by Muth, he tells me. That means that they're trimming trees directly southeast of his house, and I tell him I'll be back there directly, after I go to the bank and take care of some business. On my way to the bank, I stop by a little orchard I've established on a hill as an experiment. Some of the varieties are antique apples, like Tolman Sweets and Sops of Wine, while others are new varieties resistant to scab and other diseases. The trees are bigger now, but I've had to surround them with chicken wire to keep the deer from rubbing horns on them and chewing them down. I park the truck near a pile of dried gray applewood from the most recent orchard we've cut down, and my dog and I walk up the incline to the young trees. The wire has done its job—the young trees look like they're recovering from the earlier damage. With all the new houses being built, the deer are crowded onto our land, and destroy entire young orchards as they never did before.

The dog runs along the edge of the orchard's red-gray trees and over the golden sweet-corn stubble and green rye. We plant rye on all our sweet-corn fields and till it under each year to replenish the soil; its thin green spears are now well up across the field, while below us in another green field nearer our red fruit market building, I can see a flock of geese have landed and are honking. They eat the old sweet corn left behind after harvest. It is a cloudy day in early winter, and in the distance I can hear the roar of traffic that never ceases. Farther to the left is the golf course, and to the right, another apartment complex and a subdivision; down the road are a group of stores and a gas station. But here, on the hill, as we walk into the orchard, it hasn't changed much for more than a hundred years. Above me, a red-tailed hawk circles, and we can hear its fierce scream. Ahead of us is cornfield and orchard and woods, woods that are home to trees Michael Caples must have seen when he settled here in the 1840s. He built his cabin straight ahead, there, near where now there's the irrigation pond, blue-gray reflection on brown water.

I'll give them a hand trimming trees in a few minutes, but for now, it's enough to walk across the land accompanied by an alert black-masked border collie on a cold winter's day. Around me crowd memories of the lifetimes lived here, of workers now long dead, of children on the strawberry fields in the early summer, of my sisters Kay and Mariel and cousins Amy and Tonya picking blueberries, of relatives long since moved away or died, of story upon story, told again and again, passed down through the generations. Sometimes in solitude one is least alone. Perhaps we all are surrounded by those crowds from memory when we are in a place where such memories can still live on, a place where the past is always present. And perhaps that is what is most missing from the sterile new American landscape, devoid of farms and of lived history on the land. One day, we may well ask ourselves, not what have we gained, but what we have lost.

In the meantime, I circle around through the orchard and return to the truck, letting the dog leap up to her accustomed place on the floor. Rather than taking the highway, I cut through the back acreage on dusty two-track orchard trails, over the original fifteen acres of farmland, coming out behind the garage that we call "Paul's barn," on the other side of the paved road from Peter Joe's farmhouse. In front of me is the beautiful red barn that our grandfather, Peter Versluis, brought in from the west side of Grand Rapids board by board, beam by beam, and had reassembled here. As I pull out and drive down the road, I pass the log cabin that our grandfather had built as a memorial to his brother, Paul. In front of the cabin is a small well-house where there used to be a hand pump, and a large engraved stone. Inside the cabin, our grandfather hung various plaques memorializing the original settlers on our farmland: Tim Riley, John Cantwell, James Hagarty, Denny Caples, William Malloy, Henry Muth.

Although I don't stop, I know quite well what's inside. As you walk into the cabin, on its far side a plaque is visible. It reads: "Peter and Paul Versluis, brothers in a pleasant union for more than half a century, have been active in the honest toil of farming and fruit growing. Their children, ten and nine respectively, have been born and reared on this farm. Paul died July Four, 1955. This spot is reserved and tenderly dedicated to his memory and those who have gone on before." There are various aphorisms elsewhere on the walls, as well as a final plaque that you can see above a hand-hewn wooden table next to the door: "May you leave this cabin with a pleasant consciousness that those whom we commemorate have helped to enrich your life." It is an unusual monument for a farmer to have built, evidence here in a grove along the road of my grandfather's awareness of the past, not only of our common indebtedness to those who have gone before, but also of a sense undoubtedly felt by every generational farming family that we are but one in a long series of those who care for this place.

It is a gray day, and looks like it might rain or sleet, but as my grandfather used to say, you can't stop for the weather. I turn and drive down another orchard trail that curves past a young orchard and alongside a murky pond. I'll lend a hand trimming trees and talk with Pete, Nathan, Jim and Pete's dad while there's still time. I don't really need to go to the bank today.

# The Lay of the Land

How must it once have looked, this land, when Europeans first saw it, a scant two centuries ago. Along the Grand River were campfires and circle clearings, and then woods, trails through them that ran from fine fishing along the river, out west, one—according to an early map—right through our farm, another to our north, a silent web of foot-trails that brought one to Indian villages near the Leelanau Peninsula, or to Lake Michigan in the west. Undoubtedly we are still living off the capital that the tribespeople preserved over centuries, that capital of fine soil, woods and wildness, out of which farming is constantly born anew. I do not think we yet recognize the land's inestimable value.

It is a rolling land, wooded with oaks and maples, occasionally hemlock and pine, sometimes sandy where the ground rises, and often a heavy clay near the swamplands. There are swamplands. Indeed, to the early explorers, Michigan seemed nothing but swampland, infested, they said, by mosquitoes, flies, and other vermin, and mostly not fit for civilized habitation. Even in the nineteenth century, Emerson passed through on one of his lecture circuits and pronounced it a dreary and muddy ride. In those days, Michigan could still be considered "the West," a place for "barbarians" by comparison to cultured Boston or Concord. It was to this place that many Dutch came, among them my great-grandfather

Jacobus James Versluis on the 24th of March, 1873. In 1896, he purchased the first fifteen acres of our family's farm, today a patchwork of eighty acres here, twenty-five acres there.

To the south and to the east of our farm the land is cut by deep wooded ravines that to this day remain "the woods," dark and mysterious in their own way, home to deer herds and red and gray fox, raccoon and opossum, hawks and crows, and in the swampy lowlands, great blue herons, ducks, and sometimes, when the migratory wind is right, geese. It's as wild a land as you're likely to find so close to what passes for civilization. In places back there in the thousand acres or more of woods are precipitous holes, where the earth slopes downward out of sight among the descending trees, and far below water glints, reflecting blue, like earth's eye gazing up at the sky.

The earth drops away beneath us indeed: or rather, people relentlessly dig it out from below. Beneath those woodlands are plaster mines, shafts sunk decades ago, and in places the oak woods drop away into vertiginous sinkholes sometimes hundreds of feet wide, sloping down out of sight, as if the earth was withdrawing the woods into itself. But I can see why you wouldn't mind walking there, or riding a mule in, if you had a mule. There are other ways the earth has vanished here: some people have mined sand out of these hills that overlook the Grand River to the south, and so although you can ride or walk along the wooded ridge, you'll find that suddenly the sandy earth drops away beneath you, brown-gray root tendrils extending out into the air, drying and dying, while far below you'll see toppled trees and the flat tamped soil where the trucks ceaselessly circle, driving away with the sand that underlies the woods.

Open pit mining. Ugly words. It's a little known fact that Michigan, home to so much natural beauty, has among its tourist treasures some of America's largest open pit sand and gravel mining. Of all the things people can do to the earth, such mining has to be among the most irrevocably devastating. Not too far from our farm is a gravel pit that used to be rich river bottomland, black soil that grew melons and a few other crops. The farmer, a man I knew when I was a child, sold his mineral rights to a mining company, and is selling "lakeview" lots around the barren pit that was left behind. I remember seeing a truck go by on the highway, "BLACK TOPSOIL CHEAP" painted on its side. It seemed to sum things up well enough.

Yet the landscape remains, so that although the earth is gouged out in the river valley, the valley itself is still there, and if you were to canoe down the river, as I have sometimes done, you would be surprised at how the overarching trees along the banks, willows and, higher, elm and oak and maple, grant us the illusion that this earth has remained somehow miraculously untouched by any recent pestilence. Indeed, you might be forgiven if you were now and then to think for a moment, when the deer delicately stepped forth onto the shining soft riverbank soil and bent to drink, that some tribesman might also emerge from the brush, coming through the transparency of time like the fabled sojourner among the faery.

But on the farm you wouldn't expect such things; we live in a more prosaic world, where you spend the day borne along by the ceaseless current of labor, carrying you from one task to the next, one row to the next, over the dark earth. I began by offering images of the surrounding land because our cultivated land is woven into it, indivisibly knit, even though only the distance of memory allows one to see this. For mostly we spend our time following the day's rhythms, not thinking about the river, or the deep woods, which remain far off, a shining ribbon and darkness, simply present, the darkness out of which everything emerges and that in some mysterious ways nourishes all that we see and are.

The farm is on high land north of the river and north of the woods, a patchwork affair like most such places, bordered by suburban houses that line some streets and are scattered down others;

some land we own borders the woods to the south, but mostly it surrounds the main house on Maynard Avenue. The oldest part of the farm, just now centennial, is high, sandy, good acreage west and north of the main house. There are irrigation ponds, one in fact just south of the cornfields that slope down to the north, down to where once was swampland. Ponds like these don't have names; they just exist, some bordered by a few trees, or even woods. Everywhere on the main farm, you'll see ditches and ponds, for that's how the farm was made, by the art of drainage, as practiced by my grandfather, Peter, and his brother, Paul.

Beneath the oak and sumac east of this pond, you might find the remains of a house that once stood here, a century before, when the road ran along this ridge. Back then the roads were like our present orchard two-tracks, if that good, and it is strange to think that there once were houses and what passed for roads in places where now one sees only woods and open fields. There is even something cheering in this: one is reminded, again, of how transient human structures can be, and how they can crumble and vanish in but a few years. What was it like, living here back then? Surely it was wilderness—and yet I wonder whether there were many more animals than today. Did Michael Caples in 1848 see ever a bear, a humped black shape, from his window? Probably he, like me, saw hawks and deer, woodchucks and coon, opossum and squirrels; maybe he even saw an emerald-eyed weasel, as we did once along an orchard trail.

But the land here is defined by water, for the farm is an island amid what once were tamarack swamps. From the main barn, looking south, you'll see the blueberries, reddish branches fanned upward over the black peat and marsh water. Above them run the power lines, tall gray metal towers between which are strung the cables that power the city of Grand Rapids. In the soft spring drizzle, or in a late winter snowfall, you can hear the lines crackle overhead with the sizzle of hundreds of thousands of volts. When the power company sank the bases of those towers, the workers said that the peat muck there went down for eighteen feet. But now there is no swamp there, only sometimes standing water in the ditches, and so desiccating black soil sinks down, bit by bit, each year.

Our orchards run along the ridges and in the higher rolling land, while the flatter fields serve for sweet corn and sometimes hay. We could walk together, you and I, down these orchard trails, and I could show you where this or that orchard once was. We still call the high sandy point of a cornfield "the grapes," even though there have been no grapes there for nearly thirty years. A farm memory is a long memory; if the generational links are preserved, the names and allusions continue, richer and richer. I could imagine in a farming family centuries old that there persist living allusions to people or places or crops or events gone for hundreds of years.

It is strange how perfectly I can envision orchards and trees that no longer exist, have not existed for years. I remember, for instance, where there used to stand a black sweet cherry tree, whose trunk, by then black and grizzled, had undoubtedly been seen by my great-grandfather. This tree I vividly remember was massive, for a cherry, and on its eastern side a limb had been cut off decades before, so that out of its gray circle grew a few iridescent purple black raspberry plants. As boys we would clamber up into the tree and gorge ourselves on the sweet cherries that the birds had not yet gotten (birds are always vigilant). Does that tree still stand because it stands in our memories?

Although many farmers have cut theirs down, we still have some full-size, or standard, apple trees. A standard tree, often a McIntosh or a Northern Spy, reaches twenty feet into the air, with outstretched thick limbs bigger around than a man's leg. We've got fairly few standard trees now; our last large orchard is already on its way toward replanting, and by the time you read this, our last standard trees may well have been cut down. Some farmers trim their standard trees with a peculiar downward slant to the limbs, like weeping willows—I've seen this in Polish orchards, for instance—but like most orchards with the old full-size trees, ours are trimmed so as to create angled, jutting limbs that bear the fruit outward toward the sun.

It's true that big standard trees, having so much more leaf area, require more spraying and are harder to trim; it's true that semi-dwarf or dwarf varieties are more efficient, because you can get more trees into the same acreage; it's even true that it's far more dangerous to fall from an eighteen-foot ladder than to fall from a stepladder near a semi-dwarf tree. Nonetheless, when you walk through a standard-size apple orchard in the night, and around you are those high, bent and twisted limbs silhouetted against the starlit sky or the moon, there's a certain satisfaction that new, smaller varieties cannot offer. Here, you think, is the kind of orchard Thomas Jefferson might have tended, high and surrounding you almost like a forest—like an orderly, Dutch forest.

But much of our orchard land is devoted to new and smaller trees, more comparable when they're young to cornfields than to orchards, until the orchard grass grows into a mat, and the trees widen their grasp, expanding year by year higher and broader. A young tree lives precariously, vulnerable to all manner of predators, ranging from dolts on roaring snowmobiles who heedlessly snap off saplings, to foraging deer who like to nip back the succulent tips of the young branches, to various fungi and other kinds of infections. I suppose one could compare young trees to children: they take years to reach maturity, and all sorts of ailments or accidents might overtake them before they reach it. This is especially true of the dwarf and semi-dwarf trees, of which my Uncle Warren says their restricting roots carry with them their premature demise. But somehow, despite all the dangers, most young trees do survive and even prosper. It's a matter of grace.

Probably the greatest marvel, though, year after year, are the sweet-corn fields. People who buy sweet corn at our market or out of the stores don't realize what a feat it is to be able to offer fresh sweet corn every single day of the season, from July through September. It isn't as though one can plant a single huge field and the corn will produce continuously for months; rather, every single field has to be calculated to precede another, right up to the season's end. This is a work of intuition and engineering together: my Uncle Dave or my cousin Peter Joe have to calculate out, from late April on, each field's harvest and harvest time, all coordinated despite the vagaries of drought and deluge, of delaying cold and greenhouse heat, of marauding raccoon and birds.

These marauding birds are the result of human foolishness, for they consist mainly of redwing blackbirds, grackles, and starlings, the latter introduced into North America by some fool nostalgic for England, and nourished into huge numbers by monocultural farming. Any of these is a pretty bird on its own, but when they descend in gigantic flocks on your sweet-corn fields, just before you're ready to harvest, they take on a malevolent quality. I suppose the birds' destruction of cornfields is particularly an affront inasmuch as, unlike coon—who strip back and eat an entire ear, or at least most of it—birds will perch on a cornstalk and peck out only a single kernel, or perhaps two, then move on to another ear, and another. Every pecked ear rots. When you consider that there may be thousands of birds in a flock, you can well imagine that a single flock can destroy many acres of sweet corn just before harvest in only a few hours or less.

For a farmer who grows sweet corn, these birds are roughly equivalent to the kudzu of the South: whatever the good intentions of those who introduced them, clearly they symbolize life out of balance. Nature balances. And the greater the imbalances we humans introduce, the greater, it seems reasonable to think, the redress that nature herself will bring about. What's more, where the human population has become extremely dense, one can expect that the imbalances will be greater—and the redress more intense. Given, for instance, the massive changes in California's or Japan's landscape—the miles of pavement, the altered water table and flow, the advent of cars and airplanes, the destruction of millions of farmland acres, and all the rest—is it so unreasonable to expect that eventually the only way to restore some semblance of balance is catastrophe, be it fire, flood, earthquake, or disease? How many people, in this society so divorced from farming, could survive even a couple of months without all the apparatus of modernity, the trucks and supermarkets and all the rest? We will find out.

For this, too, is part of the land's lay, part of the meaning of the title *Island Farm*: in an indifferent and even hostile sea that's tormented by the gongs of commerce, the island remains, with its own ecology, its own watersheds and trails, its own herds of deer and coon, its own hawks and owls and fox and weasels, its own muskrat and ponds and swamps and oaks, its own apples and sweet corn, strawberries and peaches, blueberries and pears, cherries and plums, its hay and its mules and its horses. And it is an island whose shores are eroded by waves, and whose integrity is always at risk of being compromised by another marauder aiming to turn a profit. Did our grandfather know the multiple meanings of the name that he carved into that knee-high stone near the crest of the hill where stands the farmhouse that once was his?

# Ancestors

They gaze out of those nineteenth-century photographs unsmiling, almost fierce: Jacobus James Versluis and his wife, Ida; he balding, with a stripe of slicked-back dark hair in the center of his scalp, a high forehead and narrowed eyes, thin lips, wearing a black coat and small tie, rough white shirt; she plain, with small eyes, fuller lips, and a broad Dutch face; the two of them looking for all the world as if they existed out of sheer will, humorless and indomitable. Their wedding photographs were oval images set into the marriage certificate, dated 1884. So far as I know, there are not many more photographs of them. Such photographs remain one of the only traces confirming that they existed at all, other than their descendents and the farm. They were the beginning of our family line in America.

Oral family tradition has it that when James—for that's how he was known—came to these United States, arriving in the decade after the Civil War, he worked for years close to the city on a farmstead several miles away that still can be seen by its main house on the west side of Grand Rapids, albeit surrounded by city homes now. It was common then, as still today in some cultures, for a family to send over a son like James who would work and save, sending money to bring other family members to America. He and his family might well have died young in grinding poverty had they not come over to this country, and only after this undertaking was finished did he marry. Not surprisingly, the photograph doesn't reveal a romantic couple; these two were workers, who lived a difficult life with little money, but they were both generous people who did it more for family than for themselves.

It's Ida, with her slightly hooded eyes, high cheekbones, and rounded Dutch features, that most of us resemble. We know more about her than about him because she outlived him by so many years that my father, my Aunt Edith, and their siblings remember her well. Born in May of 1856, she died in December of 1947, more than thirty years after James had died. She was a strong, earthy woman, with a great sense of humor and an immense zest for life, qualities that aren't conveyed by the sober picture taken, presumably, around or before the time of her marriage on the 13th of December, 1884. She loved jokes and she loved cooking, and several times later in life she allowed whole families to come to live in her home so that they could build up savings or because they had nowhere else to turn. Aunt Edith's favorite picture shows her sitting in a chair with a Bible on her lap.

James had a good job in the city, working at Henry Smith's greenhouse on top of the Bridge Street hill near where he also had bought fifteen acres, but just after the turn of the century, he and Ida moved out to farm full-time here. It was a daring move, particularly since the farmland that he had purchased was at the time mostly tamarack swamp. There was only a narrow strip of orchard land on the original forty acres of farmland surrounding the main house—the rest was bog, all standing water and swamp grass. I think that James wanted to be his own boss, and preferred living on a relatively poor farm that he owned himself to working for someone else in a greenhouse near the city. Undoubtedly, the move into a small farmhouse on a hill surrounded by swamp probably seemed to other local farmers as only a stepping stone. Few would have thought that of all the surrounding farms, only this one would survive another century.

James and Ida had purchased the family farmhouse—located on the hill just to the west of the original fifteen acres of farmland that James had bought in 1896—from a farmer named James Hagarty. At that time the house was not very large, and that's why, when our grandfather, Peter, and his wife, Tena, took over the farm after James's death, eventually Ida went to live in a house in the city. Peter and Tena, married on the 25th of October, 1917, lived in the original farmhouse, to which they built several additions in order to house their ten children, and Peter's brother Paul and his wife and children lived in another house on the other side of the road. Their brother, Eman, was something of a black sheep in the family, sometimes living a vagabond life, and sometimes staying in the main farmhouse, where he ate meals with the family.

Paul was the older of the brothers, but it was Peter who took charge. According to my Aunt Edith, the eldest of their children and now in her eighties, the two of them were inseparable, and so far as she knew, they never had words. Paul was a gentle, good-natured and somewhat shy man, who didn't care to speak in public, while most of the children were intimidated by Peter, a burly, brusque man who took charge and made decisions with authority. Paul sold produce for over fifty years from a covered stall at the wholesale market downtown. To arrive there long before dawn, he had to awaken at 12:30 a.m., harness up a team of horses, hitch them to a loaded wagon, and drive them downtown. He did that, first with horses, later with a truck, from the age of fourteen until very near his death.

After Paul died in 1955, Peter built the log cabin down the road from the main farmhouse in fond remembrance of his brother. Inside the cabin, Peter hung plaques on which were written aphorisms like "To live without responsibility is to live without appreciation." It's a dimly lit cabin only a couple of paces across inside, and made of logs dragged out from the woods nearby, furnished with a bench and a roughly hewn small table. In front of the cabin he put an old-fashioned pumping well, so passersby could pump themselves a drink of water if they'd like; but several decades ago, someone came by and stole the pump.

On my wall now as I write is a photograph of my grandfather, standing in the field below the main farmhouse. Although I remember him as a broad-shouldered, thick-fingered man in his sixties sitting in an oaken rocking chair near the kitchen wood-stove, the photo shows a slimmer man wearing a white shirt, a tie, suspenders holding up baggy pants, and a fedora hat—not the attire one would expect for field work. He's standing in front of a workhorse in the field, his left hand lightly holding the harness reins, behind him a wooden-handled one-row cultivator. The workhorse beside him has a large, long head and a swayback; atop the horse is my Aunt Francine, at the time a girl, her little hands clasping the horse's withers. Behind him, one can see the sloping hillside of the original fifteen acres, and there's not a house in sight.

They all lived through the Great Depression of the 1930s, and my grandfather often used to drive into town with a horse and wagon in order to sell fruit to people on the west side, particularly in the Polish neighborhood. Paul took fruit to the market to sell, and according to my Uncle Dave, sometimes walked into town to take on extra work shoveling coal. During that time, almost no one had any money, and I have met more than a few people who remember my grandfather telling them that they could pay for their fruit the next week, or how much they appreciated it as children when he came through the neighborhood and they could get an apple from him. That was their treat, an elderly Polish woman told me once, a knowing glint in her eyes. People today don't believe it, but that was our treat for the week, she said. It is remarkable that my grandfather and grandmother managed to raise ten children and maintain the farm, growing potatoes and apples and berries, sweet corn and hay and peaches, during a period of such poverty.

But it was with my parents' generation that our family farm was to take on its present shape. My father went to Michigan State University and eventually got a degree in horticulture, but he also began to teach and then to become a public school administrator. So too, Uncle Phil became an administrator, in his case, director of the juvenile justice system in the county, as well as mayor of what had become the city of Walker, where most of our farm is located. Uncle Warren became a public school teacher, and Uncle Dave, the youngest of the four brothers in the family of ten, ran the farm, known as "Versluis Orchards." The four brothers all have worked on the farm on Saturdays and during the summer when it was possible, and it was the brothers who, as a partnership or individually, bought more farmland in the area when it came up for sale.

All four brothers and most of the sisters and their families built or purchased houses in the vicinity of the original farm, and it was with their children, my sisters and my cousins, that we grew up. Thus we cousins were born into a unique situation: dozens of family members within walking distance, around us orchards and ponds, woods and sweet-corn fields, blueberry bogs and strawberry patches. It was only during this period that we really began to use a lot of machinery. My father and uncles grew up plowing and cultivating with horses, just as my great-grandfather had done, but my cousins and I grew up familiar with John Deere tractors and big red spray rigs, with long trailers and pickup trucks, with motorized lifts for tree trimming and a small red International tractor for cultivating. Around us, the suburbs expanded. Times had changed.

I have often thought about the couple in those photographs on James and Ida's marriage certificate, and how astonishingly different our world is from theirs. Imagine, for instance, their amazement at our machinery, at all the devices we take for granted. This is perhaps the most surprising aspect of our technomagic: how quickly it becomes routine, almost unseen, certainly unremarked. There's a nearly miraculous quality to our machinery, because not one of us could reproduce it or even explain directly how it works: it comes into being through a whole web of mostly unexpected causes and effects, emerges into the world as a squatty green John Deere tractor, and we hop onto it as if it had always been there. One can envision a day when a boy makes his way into a dusty barn and finds in a cobwebby corner that very tractor, clambers on, and imagines what it must have been like in an era long past when people took a machine like that for granted.

For all our technomagic is ephemeral. We know this instinctively: it is no secret. Our models change from year to year, decade to decade; and we know perfectly well that our machinery is engineered to be superceded and abandoned or even to fail. On many farms, these old machines can still be found out in a field or a woods; I know, in fact, where an old horse-drawn potato planter and the remnants of a trailer rest among saplings next to a windowless green 1950s Buick. Thus the woods slowly provide cover to the metal palimpsest of a century, leaves slowly covering the rusting metal, topsoil forming along the dashboard and in the seats, the earth reclaiming what once was mined from her.

And so the farm itself remains, accepting our debris and the accumulated labor and traces of generations. This itself does not change; it was true for James Versluis near the end of the nineteenth century, and it is true for whoever will be inheriting the farm in the next century, after all a relatively short time, from the farm's viewpoint. It is often remarked that time is accelerating nowadays, and this is undoubtedly true, albeit not for the earth, not for the trees and the grass, which see things from perhaps a longer view than those of us infatuated by the whirl of lighted and roaring machinery. Indeed, it may be that even the ancestors remain, like the grass and trees, present in the landscape, in the earth and in all that they knew, loved, touched, cared for.

Certainly something of their approach to life continues into our present. I think I know what they were like, for there are family characteristics visible still; one can see the continuity from grandfather to father to son. Above all, my great-grandfather was a worker: for him, as for us, work was taken for granted, not avoided but expected, every day but Sunday. His recreation was his work. About the closest he came to leisure or a hobby was to light a fire and burn old apple tree brush, for he loved fires as much as the rest of us. An impatient man, with an implacable resolve, he could grow angry quickly, and he drove his children hard, but would show sometimes that great generosity and kindness dwelled inside that almost impermeable shell. He went to church twice on Sunday without fail, and he never cheated anyone, though he was cheated more than once. No one ever really knew him, not church members, not his children, not even his wife. No one ever really knew him because, like us, he didn't know himself—he just was.

Farming requires a certain relentlessness, one has to be able to face not only the routine of each day—the row of trees that needed trimming, the field that needs plowing or planting—but even more, the possibility and even likelihood that the crop you're tending won't make harvest, or worse, that it will be the finest crop you've ever grown, and no one will be willing to pay anything for it. Confronted by natural adversity, and human indifference, you keep going because you figure that one or another harvest is going to tide you over. And even more, you keep going because it's in your blood to do so. That's undoubtedly what my great-grandfather did, and I don't imagine that he ever saw what the world would call reward, though that's not to say he had no rewards.

In those days, you knew your neighbors, and you helped one another. We might forget, however, why this was possible if we don't recall that one can help with certain tasks only if one knows how to do them. It takes a farming family to help a farming family, and whereas in those days almost every house was a farmhouse, at least in our vicinity, today there is only one other farming family within a few mile radius: the Engelsmas. Although we know the Engelsma clan—Ted, stocky with a sunburned face, vital though he's over seventy now, is a frequent visitor at the coffee shop—we've never had much to do with them, never raised a barn or hauled hay with them, though sometimes we've passed one another on tractors or in pickup trucks.

When my father and uncles were young, during the 1930s and '40s, there were still numerous farms surrounding ours, including Malloys', Greens', Dykstras', Portfliets', Muths' and others. I have often wondered what this must have been like—though I imagine that then, as now, each family lived in its own sphere, mostly separated from the others, meeting only in rare and awkward conditions, seldom if ever just to visit, to sit together on the porch and talk about things. One family might help another now and then, but there's a sense where I'm from that each family has its own domain, and you don't cross over very much, mainly just in special circumstances, maybe weddings, mostly funerals, and every now and then, in the field, at school as boys and girls, or in a store.

You might think this insularity isn't entirely a good thing, and probably it isn't, but it does at least provide a certainty to one's world, a stability that must have seemed nigh unto permanent in those days. How many students have I taught who write poignantly of their ruined, chaotic, transient home lives, full of violence, incoherence, and grief? And our political leaders give lip service to the ideal of family stability, while fomenting policies whose main effects are the further destruction of what little agrarian stability might remain in America. Without land, without even a stable landscape, are we really to believe that people's lives can remain unchaotic? Do we not as much reflect as create our landscape?

We are hastily building a world in which generations do not know their forebears, families have no roots, and children do not grow up but merely grow, like weeds that struggle to survive in the cracks of pavement. Little wonder that to them others' lives are cheap, since their own, in dissociated urban or ex-urban squalor, are so barren. There is in America a profound rootlessness, even a kind of centrifugal force, driving people away from their forebears; it began several hundred years ago, with the separation of Europeans from their homeland, and it is paradoxically even more powerful today than in the past, almost as if it is gathering intensity as the decades pass.

Of course, there is a certain romance to this rootlessness. Films idealize it, even idolize it in flickering images that celebrate being "liberated" from the past, "liberated" from the family, "liberated" from "servitude" to the land. And no one can deny the attraction of these cinematic figures, the lone Western hero without a family or friends, just a squinty-eyed man who rides a fine horse; the beautiful woman stepping alone from a stagecoach to start a new life in a far Western town, images of people who exist without connections. It is even present in Thoreau, that iconoclast, who execrates the farmer and who calls his reader to listen to his own higher laws, to listen to his own flute playing, to wander in the woods. These are all good things, no doubt, yet one wonders if there isn't nonetheless a characteristically American exaggerated and perhaps nearly rootless plant that perhaps even Thoreau helped germinate, but that Hollywood (along with cultural disintegration and the unsettling of America) brought into full bloom. I think it may be a variant of nightshade.

One could not expect an American ancestor worship, an elevation of great-grandparents into a pantheon of some kind, but along the way on this trajectory towards solipsism—where everyone has his own individual satellite or starship, replete with repellers—some of us might want to get off, landing gently on the earth to which we belong by birth. Most dangerous in the contemporary situation is isolation not only from nature and from one another, but from our past, from all those who have gone before, and who represent our hereditary link to one another and to our world; they are our invisible community, among us by absence and presence both, through hidden traces that manifest in who and where we are now. I do not think we realize how much we live on the intangible riches gathered by our ancestors; often I think that we are bent upon exhausting every last bit of the treasures they accumulated over millennia in a bizarre frenzy of selfish indulgence.

I wonder if those who are so intent on selling off to the highest bidder all that they have been given would act the same could they hear or see around them the concerned, grieving, perhaps even wrathful countenances of their ancestors gazing at them from the invisible. For we are surrounded by those who came before; they permeate their legacies to us. Such legacies are not only physical, not only ancestral lands, but also all that they have bequeathed to us; not only what they owned or cherished (for can we really own anything? If so, who is so permanent on this earth as to keep anything?) but even our features and our characters, how we are and who we are; and even more than this, that grand unseen inheritance of understanding, of words and songs and attitudes, of philosophy and spirituality, of all that gives life meaning.

Americans, I think, want to live as though they have no ancestors, no obligations, no responsibilities; it is part of the national character, and though this attitude generates that refreshing perpetual newness so entrancing to those who perceive themselves as entrapped by tradition, it has its consequences. We hear much talk about ecology and "saving the world" nowadays, but frankly, it is only talk, for so long as people choose to live as if they are disconnected from one another and from the past—and is this not the genesis of the so-called "American dream?"—there is no such thing as an authentically ecologically balanced way of life, and there is no "saving the world."

Perversely, the word "conservative" has somehow been co-opted by the advocates of *maschinenzivilisation*, the advocates of the abstract over the tangible, of the corporation and the corporate over the individual and the local, of exploitation and exhaustion over renewal and continuity. What does it really mean to "conserve?" Surely it has nothing to do with the avaricious, self-serving proclamations we hear from those who have assumed the label but not the reality. Bound up in all this is precisely the question of ancestors, and of our responsibility to maintain and augment, rather than use up, what we have been given. Surely there is little "conservative" in those who insist that the marketplace determines all values. It doesn't. The marketplace is all that's left at the bottom of an empty barrel when meaning has been emptied out.

For life is given meaning only through connection. A symbol connects a lower and a higher mode of being; and our religions and philosophies, our literatures and sciences and arts, all are conveyed through symbols. Where do these symbols come from? Dreams and visions, to be sure, and imagination, the fountain of creativity. But only to the degree that we are connected to our past, to the vast treasures given us by our ancestors, genetic and otherwise, do these symbols take on full meaning. The richest works of art are those most illuminating, in a new way, of all that we have already been given, just as the most fertile farm is so because of the accumulated efforts of generations, whose eyes are always set on improving life for those who will come after. This is connection, and without it, there isn't conservatism, only self-aggrandizement at the expense of those to come.

*Island Farm* signifies an understanding of these truths. Exemplary of this middle way is my father, who has planted more trees and flowers on his land than anyone I know. It's said that one would have to plant nearly seven hundred trees to compensate for the pollution of one automobile over a ten-year period, and my father is one of very few people I know who can say that he has planted that many trees and more on his property. Now, in the spring and summer, you'll see black-barked pines and gray-barked oaks encircling his land and his house, so much so that from a few hundred feet away, you can't see his house at all. And if you were to come closer and walk among those trees, you'd see all manner of wildflowers blooming, white with red tongues, yellow, red, blue, also bushes with red berries, cedar, birch with white and black papyrus bark, hemlock, and grapes.

This planting is what wise ancestors do—and that's what we ought to do as well, we who will one day after all *be* ancestors. Perhaps this is the most alarming aspect of contemporary American life: that people live not only as if they had no ancestors, but worse, as if they were not going to be anyone's ancestors. Surely this is one way of seeing the American infatuation with mobility, with mobile homes and automobiles, with disposable stores and disposable plastic trinkets to sell in those stores. Evidently, we long to live as if we were not related to anyone or anything. We want to discard everything, even our past. There is an intoxication with blaming one's family or ancestors for all that befalls one now, and while often there's some truth in such revelations, on the whole we've been given more than we want to let on, and even if we haven't, we can still create something enduring for those to come.

Perhaps this is the deepest betrayal by those who would sell land to the highest bidder, who eagerly, childishly, thoughtlessly want to nail together another lifeless apartment complex or another strip mall on this rich and precious oasis of land in a desert already cluttered with the carcasses of such buildings. Such people betray both their link with the past and their link with the future; and as I look at this oval photograph of my stern great-grandfather and great-grandmother, gazing out from a time so remote that they might have lived in another world entirely, I know well enough what my great-grandfather would say to those people. The nineteenth-century Germany theosopher Franz von Baader wrote that a moral decision will either shame us or shame others, and perhaps there's some truth in that. May this landscape loved by so many in the past be loved also in the future, for that more than any other is the tie that binds us to what has been, what will be, and above all, to what matters.

# Childhood

A child is walking down an orchard trail, and all the trees are in bloom. It's sunny, and the spring water is rushing in the earth's veins, the soil glistening in the bright light; he hears bees in the white blossoms overhead, reaches down to feel the shining soft brown mud, runs ahead to grasp his father's hand. His eyes dart up to see the circling hawk that his father points toward, high over the orchard's green canopy; he walks with a child's swaying, an innocent swagger, drinking everything in. What does he see? Feel? Hear? Is everything brighter, sharper for him than for us? Who is he, already?

Some claim that childhood is a kind of paradisal state, and perhaps in some sense it is. But as we grow older, we forget what our childhood was like; it becomes enshrouded in our later memories, foggy and distant, images of the past that we only glimpse, this memory, or that one. I doubt most adults remember much of anything about childhood. We recall one image or another, but we're adults now, and mostly these early memories remain ensconced in deeper geological layers of the mind. Few of us can see deeper than the dust that's settled recently, far less the deep strata revealed in the colors of a mind's canyons. Is this perhaps a blessing?

I'm not claiming I was reared in paradise—far from it. But when I was growing up, our world seemed stable. Our extended family is vast—my grandfather and grandmother had ten children, and they in turn married and had children, and most of their children in turn married and had children. So you can imagine what one of our family reunions is like: row after row after row of tables, and I mean long tables. There were and are family disagreements, but there was a sense of community that still exists. And no one ever said that they expected this world would be destroyed; not a single acre of our family's farmland was sold for suburban housing; we lived on a farm, and that was that.

Across the swamp and up on the ridge near the storage is my Uncle Warren and Aunt Glady's farmhouse, behind which were the old McIntosh apple trees, intermingled with some Spies on the far end. As a boy, those trees seemed gigantic, and compared to today's varieties, they are, for they stand twenty-five feet or more in the air, their gray arms outstretched. I remember riding on my father's lap on a tractor as we drove through the orchard; I remember when there were peach trees there along the ridge, and how my father and uncles would pick them into peck baskets for our fruit stand. To the east, across the sweet-corn fields and past the orchards is my Uncle Phil and Aunt Joyce's house; to the south are the homes of other aunts and uncles, all on the periphery of the family farm's gentle hills and ridges.

Uncle Dave's house was right next door, and I remember often him shouting over the horse pasture fence for my father, who would go walking across the pasture in the evening. They'd stand along that fence and talk about some decision, maybe tell some story about what happened that day. In those days, my father smoked a pipe, and so you'd smell that burley tobacco in the air; and sometimes my father would come putt-putting along on a small red Farmall tractor to cultivate the garden. As a child, I lived an insular life in a world where adults did their inscrutable ordinary adult things, and we children played, ran among the brown pine needles, under the green of the white pines and oaks. We had no cause to worry.

It was not a magical world. Kathleen Raine has written of her magical childhood, and many others have written along such lines, but that's not the world I remember. There's not much faith in magical worldviews for most moderns, and Calvinists are not excepted—far from it. We are a prosaic and empirical bunch, bent on work. Still, childhood was a realm hermetically sealed, mostly, from that of adulthood; the adult world was that of the Olympian gods, who would intervene in our lives when necessary. It's easy to idealize childhood, I think, and just as easy to dismiss it, as W. C. Fields did with the quip that anyone who hates children can't be all bad. But the truth lies somewhere between the two, as it always does.

Certainly we played. My cousin Peter Joe, a year older and blond like me, used to come by from next door, and we'd play Daniel Boone and Mingo, or something else that required us to act as though we were living in another century. Under the black-barked pine trees, we'd track Indians through the brown bed of fallen needles, and I remember well enough tracing out a moccasin print in the moist brown dirt with an extended forefinger, as well as pitched battles with invisible foes whose fierceness was met full force by our own. Such play means that though one knows one isn't living in wilderness, wilderness it becomes nonetheless, fed by magnificent cinematic images of mountain men like Jeremiah Johnson lingering in our memories. All our lives are like this: for as adults, we still transform our worlds, and ignore what we do not want to see. Perhaps, too, that wilderness is still there, whether we see it or not.

All around us were adventures. Nearby were the horse pastures, and on the other side of the page-wire fences were orchards in one direction, open fields in another, and to the north, a swamp that in those days still had standing water in it. Many's the adventure we had wandering through the swamps and fields and nearby woods. I recall finding a nest of raccoons in a hollow tree, their black-ringed brown eyes gazing out at us, as curious as our own eyes looking in. My sisters were always finding birds or other animals to rescue, bringing in baby robins and obnoxious grackles, whatever happened to have been separated from its mother. Sometimes distant relatives came to visit in the summer, and I remember one, my Aunt Lisa, who ended up raising a pet raccoon. We went to school, of course, but I have little recollection of that, for the real learning took place outside.

When I grew older, too old to play as children do, I entered books for the first time, and here began another kind of play, one whose delights I still enjoy. Emerson may have been right to scorn fiction, but a child's imagination is nourished by stories. Asthmatic as a boy, I lived more than most in a literary world, a world of words and dreams of all kinds; I was voracious for fields where the mind could gambol. There is great wisdom in the tales of Michael Ende, who keeps alive faith in the imagination with fantastic works like *The Neverending Story*. The imagination is indeed threatened by the encroaching nihil of artificial stimulation, and must be nourished by the magic of stories and encouraged dreaming.

What stories? I read everything: the Great Brain and Doc Savage, *Thousand and One Tales*, Robert Louis Stevenson, C. S. Lewis and Tolkien, books on all manner of things. Once I conceived a fascination for hypnosis, and at thirteen or fourteen commenced collecting what I could find on the subject—I still have *Animal Hypnosis* by a Russian author. The idea that one could hypnotize birds was especially attractive to me for some reason, but alas, I never had a chance to try it out on our chickens, inasmuch as Rebel, my mother's horse, in his turn took a fancy to trampling underfoot whatever hapless chickens flapped their way into his pasture. They rarely flapped back out, instead becoming one with the soil and hooves, and so soon I didn't have chickens to hypnotize. But I did have books, and I read them all: old Hardy Boys adventures and tales of Canadian Mounties, Sherlock Holmes mysteries, anything I could lay hands on.

My two sisters and I worked on the farm in the early summer mornings, sometimes, picking strawberries, and here we came to know the other cousins, boys and girls both. Picking strawberries meant that you'd spend the morning kneeling beside or bent over your row, and if there was dew, your hands would grow pale and wrinkled as you slowly filled your quart boxes. But the money wasn't all of it: you also would be sitting among other children, and that in itself was an education. Unlike school, where there was relatively little time or encouragement for talking or for just being alone while you worked, amid the snapping sound of berry stems separating you could become involved in a long conversation, or speak to no one at all. There was always something going on—a surreptitious berry fight, a flirtation, a quarrel, competition to fill quarts, gossip.

Yet there was a day when the shadow of the Fall from the Garden crept over us more darkly than usual. It was a sunny, warm day, children picking across the field, my uncle standing watch, a few of us packing berries from the wooden carriers, when we heard a rumble in the distance along with a crackling sound. A fine mist drifted over the strawberry field, and there was a peculiar sulphurous smell in the air. Perhaps this was what it was like in Vietnam when the soldiers came into a farming community—it was roughly the same era. For over the hill came a strange-looking tank-treaded machine, a sloping futuristic thing like a crane with no boom, along with it two men in what appeared to be sullied white space suits, carrying spray guns attached to a sloshing spray-tank by long black hoses. The apocalypse comes not with four horses but with horsepower.

They cracked and crunched their way under the power lines that adjoin our farm and bisect it further to the east, around them a mist and a foul chemical smell that belonged then and still belongs to another world than ours, to Detroit or to Gary, Indiana, to places where yellow air and alien chemical smells are commonplace, even expected. They blasted jets of a chemical closely related, I much later discovered, to the notorious Agent Orange used during the Vietnam War, killing all the foliage under the power lines so that nothing might grow up and one day touch those corded lines that hum and crackle with the city's power. Some of my cousins talked to the sprayers, who idled their alien machine and spoke casually, leaning against it like chemical cowboys, husky tanned college boys out working a summer job. Behind them the greenery wilted, sickened, died a brown death in a swath miles long.

Perhaps most strange to me now is our indifference. We all took for granted this emergence from over the hill of some alien machine run by aliens, accepted it with no more concern than those college boys who did the spraying, accepted it as we accepted the power lines themselves, those great gray metal towers that run electricity across the land and bring to the city that nightly glow, its fragile artificial halo. Who wonders at the presence of such things anymore, at either the miracle or the monstrosity of them? As children, we picked our berries, we got our nickel a quart, and we played our games, lived out our intrigues, just like the adults, while beside us all ran the machines that kept nature at bay—not in some distant jungle land, but right here at home. What we call civilization rests solely on the casual indifference to even the monstrous, inculcated since childhood. In the end, it is probably not a very sturdy pedestal.

But this was just a shadow cast over us one morning, and it passed as do all such shadows, as do all clouds. Perhaps one meaning of Christ's admonition to become as little children is visible here: as children we spent no energy on investigation or judgment of such events, but only watched them as we watched everything else, with curious eyes. And maybe wisdom means coming around to this same attitude once again, learning to see things as they are, clearly, without fear or expectation. What did we learn from picking strawberries? That your legs often got sore, that your hands became red-stained, and that if you picked hard and long without talking, you'd make more money. But it was hard-earned money.

We also learned the value of perseverance in those days, even perseverance under unpleasant conditions like thunderstorms. For on some ill-starred cloudy days the sky to the west grew lower and the wind blew ceaselessly from the east, sometimes thunder rumbled in the distance, lightning flickered between sky and earth. But usually we kept on picking, kept on packing our berries in wooden crates or later in cardboard flats. Sometimes we'd ready a canvas to throw over the berries already picked, but that was the extent of our preparations.

And my Uncle Warren, a big, tall man who taught junior high during much of the school year, would stand watch over the pickers, sometimes kneeling and rustling his thick fingers through the green leaves behind this or that picker, revealing a new cache of red, ripe berries. When the thunder grew impossible to ignore, he'd look to the west, and you'd hear his bass voice rumble too, as he said those immortal words: "It's just a passing cloud." Even nowadays, when we are out in the field picking sweet corn, peaches, or apples and a torrent of rain breaks from the sky, someone will repeat this expression and we know that we'll return home wet to the skin.

We persevered through many a passing cloud, through many a downpour. As my grandfather would say, "You can't stop for the weather," and of course we rarely would. Only imminent lightning would drive us from a field; we'd cast apprehensive glances toward the west or northwest as we picked, watching the flashes grow brighter and nearer, until finally we knew for certain that the passing cloud was going to pass right over our heads and perhaps fry us in the bargain. Then we'd hastily stack the carriers on the trailer and drive off, some children wavering along on bicycles, some sitting around the trailer's edge, some following behind. I remember once or twice lightning striking trees nearby as we drove off amid a thunderous downpour, everyone instinctively flinching as the white blast shook the ground beneath us. But we always made it back to the barn, albeit soaking wet.

Inside the barn or the shed we'd sit while the rain came down in roiling, whipping curtains that, with the gusts, spattered even inside on the dirt floor. Parents idled their cars along the roadway or in the drive as the children ran to them, but my cousins and I, my uncles, and Jim Van Dyken, we'd sit inside, lounging against the machinery or propped up against thick-ribbed tractor tires as the rain drummed against the metal roof. It was boring. We might have a bit of idle conversation. Eventually there'd be some horse-play, a tussle, and then we'd notice that the rain was diminishing to fitful squalls. After a rainstorm, before the light breaks through the clouds everything glistens, the grass and the trees look luminous and glow greenly, lighted from within by the lightning's passing and the water.

Or perhaps I would walk home through the rain, change into dry clothes, and read for a while, the dryness of the book's pages somehow more pronounced against my wet, wrinkled fingers. Off into imagination's realm, through the dry white portal of a book, beyond the ornate, black and white letters like the frame of a mind's door into the sphere of images and fantasies. Perhaps it is too easy, as an adult, to forget the transport of reading, that mysterious passage into other worlds and times; we grow inured as adults, enwrapped in our cocoons of worry, and don't remember what it means to read. Reading can be a spiritual discipline too, our entry into countless mysteries, but only if we can, like children, live among the spaces between words, leap the gap between two minds or, put another way, leap into a consciousness that two or more can share.

I have always thought that there should be a balance between the world of imagination and the world of cold, pale, wrinkly hands and damp knees in the straw. Both are a necessary part of life, and if a Dutch upbringing often lacks the former, the latter is also crucial. In fact, when I remember childhood, I remember these two side by side, almost like living in different worlds through which we effortlessly pass, and that interpenetrate and illuminate one another. There is the world of the farm, and there is the world of books. Perhaps the richness of life comes from both, like the *vesica piscis* where two circles overlap. In this fish-shape, that primordial symbol of Christianity, the worlds meet— the social-natural, and the imaginative-divine—and life takes on new color.

A child lives to soak up experience, but increasingly, an American childhood means that one grows up in isolation, with a television and, perhaps, local hoodlums. I have taught students who had never been outside their city during their entire childhood, whose treeless, arid world of blowing trash and cracked concrete was populated by thugs whose only culture was violence, and where children only occasionally found precarious shelter from the bloodshed and hopelessness. Sometimes that shelter was not even in their own home, but that of some relative, and one can only marvel at the resilience of those who grow up in such a place but do not become themselves monstrous.

We are all diminished by a world that contains such wasted lives. But there is more that can be said about this. Why is it that Americans are willing to offer lip service for preserving family farms, lament the urban wastelands in which children are languishing and dying, and yet affirm economic and social forces that are responsible for the destruction of the farms and the creeping devastation of the cities? These things are linked, you see. They have their common origin in the misguided belief—vaunted by those who call themselves conservatives but do not conserve—that everything has only a monetary value, and that the "free market" should be arbiter of our lives' every aspect. I know all too well the evils of totalitarianism, but it's obvious that our modern econotheism, our worship of economics (wrongly and narrowly defined as the monetary system), is sucking the life out of both rural and urban America.

Yet as children, we knew nothing of these things; we did not even notice the creeping of the city outward, the slow encroaching of the suburbs upon us. To us, life on the farm was a given; we never gave a thought to what we had all around us because, perhaps like all children, we knew nothing else. We lived on a farm where the dusty orchard two-track trails ran in the same places year after year; we took for granted the certainty of what surrounded us, just as we took for granted that spring followed winter. We rode ponies through the fields and orchards all year long; we picked strawberries and blueberries in summer, and rode atop trailers laden with stacked bales of hay; life unfurled around us much as it must have for our grandfather and for our parents, much as it does for anyone born to a farming family.

Occasionally, we did recognize that we were being surrounded by those who didn't participate in or even recognize our world. I remember more than once when neighbor children dumped over and destroyed bins of apples; and I remember well seeing others scampering away from our orchards at harvest time, carrying off bags of stolen apples. Once, I recall, we caught a young man with a paper bag, and in it were tiny green apples that wouldn't be ripe for another two months. But the truth is, we had relatively little of that, and if across the highway a grocery store replaced a marsh, or if down the street numerous homes were packed into a subdivision, those were things we didn't take much notice of, for they didn't seem to concern us. The city still seemed to us much farther away than it really was.

All the themes and patterns of our lives are given us in the beginning, and life is their panoramic unfolding. Childhood, it seems to me, is like the germinating plant, and only with the plant's withering and dying again into the soil do we see the whole cycle, see what it was, what fruit it bore, how green and rich it stood, embracing the sun's light. Some people come to life in richer fields, ancient souls who bear treasures from who knows what distant clime, and you know this intuitively from them even when they are still children. It is important to see our life's meaning in where we are from, in what soil we grew, and why the wind blew our seed to this place and not that. Perhaps such an affirmation is a necessary part of maturing, for it reveals to us the enigma of our life's beginning, always bearing in embryo the mysterious possibilities we are born to realize.

Thus life is both a dream and an awakening, a *coming to*. We shake off the sleep of centuries as we come to, surprised as we begin to realize where and who we really are. It is sad to think of children awakening in a world without those adventures of childhood, without the little crick out back where the crawfish crawl in the springtime, without the open fields and the tall orchards, without the scream of the hawk overhead and the widening circle left by a diving muskrat, without the rows of strawberries in which to pick, without the tap-tap of woodpeckers in the swamp, and the loose-legged fawn's first steps through the grass, without all the beauty of a blooming orchard in springtime.

I wonder now about that little blond boy, walking along with his father through that orchard on a sunlit spring day under a vast blue sky. Who can tell what adventures life will bring him? A child is living possibility, a cipher whose life is in its own unveiling, intricate music whose measures are variations on a theme, resonating for all around him. How foolish is a way of life that seeks immediate self-profit at the expense of the children to come! What father, when a child asks him for bread, would give him only a stone? And yet that is what we do all too often in the name of "progress." If we were to somehow, miraculously, change how we saw the world, perhaps the only true measure of that change's wisdom would be whether what we then did was good for our children's children's children's fullness of life, for that child walking in an orchard many centuries from now.

# Lions, Tigers, Snakes

An August evening in Michigan like any other: in the distance the hum of traffic and closer in, the occasional flicker of a firefly, the evening star emerging in the blue-black sky, and the humidity dense as a cloud, the apple trees swollen with fruit and the peach trees divested of theirs. Night moves imperceptibly over the farm, and far off one hears unfamiliar sounds. Sitting on the porch, we cock our heads and listen: it is no siren, nor any honking horn, not even some exotic bird, but something else, closer perhaps to thunder. Thunder? And suddenly we recognize it: those are the throaty roars of lions and tigers from a neighboring farm. The circus people have come back again.

When I was growing up, a neighboring farm owner often lent his land to a traveling circus, giving them a place to rest during their peregrinations across America. And so whenever we heard that sound of lions' and tigers' roars reverberating in the warm August evening, we'd know that in the next day or two, or perhaps that very night, if we walked along the orchard trails and under the power lines we'd come to the long white barn with its green shingled roof, and all along it would be cages upon wheels, motor homes, long electrical cords as thick as your thumb snaking along the ground. You'd hear the grumbling lions first, but as you came closer you'd hear the leaping monkeys chattering, and perhaps as you stood there on the periphery along with the other children and occasional adults, you'd see the acrobats or clowns practicing.

How strange, now that I think about it later, that these exotic animals and people were so close to our farm: we almost never went to the circus, because each summer the circus came to us. And there we'd stand, watching fascinated as the tigers paced to and fro in their little cages, looking as uncomfortable as we felt in our cinderblock schools. I remember being surprised that the tigers' skins were so loose: we wondered if you could pull it into a bunch like an unmoored carpet. The lion-tamers sometimes would drive their captives into a larger, fenced arena by means of wire tunnels, and have them leap gingerly onto pedestals, all the while shouting their training commands or cracking their whips.

What creatures and people there were! There were thickly gray-skinned elephants that lumbered about, gazing at us with their rheumy eyes, sometimes drinking water with a delicacy that belied their immensity. There were monkeys and snakes and white horses, and always there were people who in a show undoubtedly would wear spangly tights, but who when we saw them wore athletic suits and ordinary clothing that somehow made their presence even more peculiar, as though our neighbors had suddenly taken to tiger-taming and sword-swallowing. These people, handsome and well-muscled, always ignored us, sternly watching their animals, or practicing their acrobatics as if we weren't there, and as if they weren't on a farm's gravel driveway, but were in a show for the Prince of Monaco.

We'd stand ringed around them in silence as they worked, the lion-tamer cracking his whip and demanding that the recalcitrant cats perform as they balked, shook their heads, snarled, and then leaped, muscles rippling under slack tan fur; the monkeys clambering up and down, some wearing costumes, like pinafores and hats, scrunching up their dark faces and grimacing or screeching; an elephant lumbering past with a woman on its back. And then some of us would look cautiously into the remaining cages, where a mottled python or a boa constrictor lay curled up, and we'd wonder what sort of life these poor creatures led, shunted from city to city and paraded in front of crowds. Eventually we realized that the exotic is only tawdriness seen from afar.

But the circus's presence, in those days a local secret, did for one remarkable summer become more than a local event—it gained international notoriety. Perhaps you recall when it happened: it made all the papers. I'm referring, of course, to the summer that the eighteen-foot-long python Big Sid escaped into the wild. No one is quite sure how it happened, or at least no one is telling: probably some employee left a cage ajar, or untended. But on and off that whole summer there were teams of local volunteer fire department people out looking in the fields and woods adjoining our land—paunchy, balding men trudging through the brush and scanning the brown grass for a glimpse of that python.

Naturally, they found nothing. Certainly people were on the alert: every few days the local paper ran an article on the wily python loose in the suburbs that surrounded our farm: parents kept their children close, lest Biff or Muffy become a telltale bulge in the python's middle; and because there was a small reward for his capture, the snake was hunted occasionally—but unsuccessfully—by locals. Mostly life went on just like it did every summer, but when we trimmed trees, we did hope that one day we'd see a long, mottled critter as thick as your leg descending an apple tree near us. We hoped, but we never did see it.

For my part, I felt a certain sympathy for that snake. Imagine what it would be like, first to be kidnapped by this traveling circus, and then to escape into a wholly alien landscape. Talk about a Gnostic allegory! Surely that was an Ophite mystery drama, that escape of the python into suburban America—the snake in the garden, this time to devour someone's French poodle out on a lawn, rather than conveying knowledge to Eve or to Adam. Surely, too, the python must have found ours a peculiar place, with no familiar game to hunt, nor any familiar trees to climb, much as if you or I were to find ourselves on some distant planet.

And of course, I feared for the snake. For I know the ways of men in my region, and they are not likely to greet a python, however harmless or disoriented it might be, with a plate of milk and a gently warmed rat. Much more likely was the python to be met with multiple blasts from half a dozen shotguns, after which whatever was left would be mounted in some fellow's living room over his fireplace. Then too, there was the enormous likelihood that the python would make his way onto a road to absorb some warmth, only to find himself flattened by a speeding car or truck. If he slithered as far as the highway, he undoubtedly would have met such an end, without even a moment to luxuriate on the hot asphalt.

In fact, this latter possibility itself gave rise to an enterprise that lasted on and off for that entire summer: some local youths discovered that a black corrugated plastic sewer pipe, marked with a few strategic pieces of masking tape at odd angles and dragged across a road at night in front of an oncoming car, created a terrific stir in the community. This faux Big Sid gave rise, so I gather, to a number of python sightings during those summer evenings: out would come the fire engines and the official cars, the burly, swaggering policemen, the volunteer firemen and their searchlights, out wading through grass and marsh water looking for that wily python, which somehow eluded them every time.

I well remember standing atop an orchard hill in the darkness, above us the stars' canopy, already drops of dew forming on the grass, watching the dim forms of police and firemen and strutting city officials, the gathering headlights down below us, the flashing searchlights, hearing the shouts of men in the field. All this labor to capture a python that would surely die if left alone until winter, all this labor so that four or five men could finally grasp that snake's thick and cool body, hauling him back to his glassy captivity, all this labor to return the unexpected wild to the world of order and safe gawking.

Indeed, when finally the python was captured and held triumphantly by seven men (among them my Uncle Warren) I was a bit saddened. If the snake had been captured and returned to a snake's paradise, why, that would have been one thing, but perhaps it enjoyed its adventure in those Michigan swamps and woods and orchards, its freedom to hunt and to sunbathe and to slither wherever it wished. I know, in any case, that its presence in our countryside gave me a certain pleasure: it was good to know that there was an actual predator out in the countryside, a Grendel of a python that meant you couldn't walk through the marsh sawgrass without casting a wary eye to either side.

We are too accustomed to our familiar suburban landscapes and to our cocoons of metal and plaster, of wood and of entertainment, our habitual patterns of life that leave no room for the unpredictability of wildness and dreams. We need a python now and then. When the python escapes into our lives, life reveals its dreamlikeness, the jarring strangeness of the wholly unexpected and even of the holy. I am reminded of Latin American and Eastern European fiction, which tends toward the magical and strange: this is how the holy is too, in this world, rupturing our habits and shattering our routines, illuminating our lives with an unfamiliar light, revealing once and for all whether we have lived with honor or tedium, whether we are truly men and women, or are ourselves living as if asleep.

There was a time when one could expect a black bear to emerge into a clearing, when one might see a lynx in our part of the state, but in our current landscape of carefully surveyed quadrants, these predators are long gone. To fly over Michigan, as over almost any part of settled America, is to see below a familiar and endless series of squares from which the unpredictable has been, as much as possible, eliminated. The last black bear and the last lynx in my homeland were shot long ago, though their brethren still can be found up north. We have lost something. Wildness means that there is also danger: there are creatures in the woods that we can't control, that emerge from a sphere we can enter truly only when we leave behind our carefully defined squares and boxes.

Perhaps it takes a jungle reptile escaping into our swamps to restore to our lives at least something of this unfamiliar wildness. But consider our reactions to it. Just as we do with deer and bear and raccoon and ducks and geese and even squirrels, we hunted it down. We took to the fields in long rows of tramping men and talked to one another on our crackling radios, flashed our brilliant searchlights and poked the grass with our long sticks; we flew over the trees and marshgrass with helicopters and drove about on all-terrain vehicles and motorcycles; we posted rewards and we enlisted the help of countless strangers. Why? To restore order, of course. To eliminate the strange. It was inevitable: we could not think of doing anything else.

But of course the strangest part of my story is the snake's presence to begin with, the snake and the circus it came from. There is something peculiarly American in this modern circus, in the pizzazz and razzle-dazzle of it, the glittering sequins and the beasts brought in from the far corners of the earth so that they could lumber or leap onto plastic ottomans, be gazed and gawked at, live their lives inside wire mesh or under glass, on the road. It is an alluring and alarming symbol, this carnival exhibiting our ability to ship jungle creatures into the north and make them gambol for us. The artifice of its "death-defying thrills" bears underneath it the sad fact of animals and people whose only home is the road, detached utterly from their native land and put on display for our diversion, as the python was after his capture. Several weeks later, he died.

No, I sympathize with that snake who escaped into our marshes and woods and orchards. He only sought a home, a familiar place, and is this not what Americans themselves all too often lack? Those fields and orchards are written in my soul: I can walk them in my mind's eye, in an instant seeing the hillside and that orchard with its tall standard apple trees, limbs outstretched like arms open to the sky, seeing that wall of dark woods and the tangled dense brown swamp grass atop which is this year's green, through which mice dart, while in the brown waters muskrat navigate. In the dog days of summer it must have seemed a python's paradise, our steamy heat and the swamp's dank breath awakening ancestral memories of his native land.

But what is our true native land? Are we still, like that escaped python, living in an unfamiliar land whose inward nature we do not really know at all? It takes many generations before people come to truly know a place. I think that our family, here for more than a century, is becoming familiar with this earth; seeing crops growing on different fields year after year, one slowly comes to learn what can grow in this soil and in that. But there is something beyond this in belonging to a place, something inward and holy. In many American Indian tribes, as in Australian Aboriginal traditions, you are seen to have a special, sacred connection to your birthland. If we Americans in general lack this, surely we are missing something profound, perhaps even something of what it means to be human. Are we not all called to become indigenous?

But alas, our farm, like so many others, also has some similarity to that poor python in that it too is hunted. True, we do not have platoons of men treading over our landscape, an occupying force—our siege is economic. Our opponents raise the flag of "progress," cry havoc and let loose the dogs of financial war. And in present-day America, this mercantilism reigns. If land is worth more as a gravel pit, a strip mine, a toxic waste dump, or an apartment complex, why, then, should it remain farmland? There is in this mercantile code no room for higher values, for how can you quantify meaning? How much money is the sight of tasseling sweet corn worth? An apple tree festooned with white blossoms?

Few things are more pernicious to human life than the reduction of everything to money.

Ultimately a farm is sustained in the human community by its inward value; it subsists by our care, as on nature's and God's grace. A farm isn't a factory, and it isn't disposable. And in the end, it isn't much like an escaped python, either. A farm is a place where people grow, each year, to understand more deeply who and where they are. A farm means connections: if soul is joined to the body by a silver cord, we are each joined to one another and to the land in countless intricate patterns of silvery sublunary strands, ties that join us to everyone else and to every living thing we are bound to care for. There are those who would say that freedom comes from the absence of responsibility, but in truth freedom comes in the fulfillment of responsibility, through which we become who we really are.

Circuses and circus people are fascinating, and there's a special fascination too in life on the road. Indeed, one of my closest friends is nomadic by nature, and through him, by contrast to him, I have come to understand what it means to be agrarian. We agrarians mark changes not by movement through space, like nomads, but by movement through time, by the slow and ceaseless turning of the seasons and the years. Though I have traveled much, I have always known where home was, and never lost inner sight of that familiar landscape whose lineaments are before me now in the clear blue and golden light of late summer harvesttime. We need one another, nomads and agrarians, for the truth is: even circus people need a farm to come home to.

# Youthful High Spirits

I don't know about you, but when we were growing up, we never worried much about consequences, we just did things. If we thought of it, we generally did it, a philosophy that, however admirable for its activeness, has certain drawbacks, chiefly revealed when one gets caught. I grew up with my cousins, among whom were Peter Joe, Steve, Peter Phil, Chad, Dan, and then among the younger boys Henry, Bill, Vince, Nathan. As you can imagine, this meant that when we got together, there was already a crowd, and a tendency toward violating rules and laws.

It's strange to recall how life was in those days, because now it all seems as if it were a dream, like a film you might have seen years ago. Where is the childhood that we scarcely have time to remember? Surely there's little clearer evidence of life's transience; it is as though we were each actors in a drama staged long ago, and although we walk about on the set, even it is under construction, and not the same as we recall it. Even personalities can change, ebullient boys becoming sober men, and it is as if the ebullience were someone else's, in another age. And yet you can trace the threads back, see the boy within the man through imagination's window.

Peter Joseph and I grew up near each other and though it's true that a house next door might as well be a mile or a light year away, still we played together; learned to read together; learned to parse mathematical calculations through games my mother devised (mainly because the local school system was closer to a set of walls in which we children were confined during the day than to a place of education); worked together; and raised havoc together, along with the rest of the wild bunch.

It's interesting to think how far apart houses can be from one another, however close they might appear, each one a kingdom unto itself. Perhaps this is something characteristic of American life more generally, this rural or suburban isolation, each home silent to others, connected only by thin wires and rare visitors. In the old days, and in some churches still, church elders would visit homes and, in the stiffly formal sitting room—children dressed up, the men in suits and ties, women in starched dresses—they would talk uneasily about whether anyone had fallen away, but mainly about the weather or crops or maybe some gossip. Nowadays, even this contact is gone, and it's rare for anyone to visit another's home save on the holidays. This is far from the Old World, where grand-children, children, parents, grandparents, uncles, aunts, all might live under the same roof, or in adjoining houses.

But when my cousins and I were growing up, our families were all within a mile radius of one another, on different parts of the farm, and we all took this communion of souls for granted. Only when I went off to college did I realize how rare this is in America, how much closer it is to an Old World way of life, and how fortunate we were. For think of what it required: first the great spread of farmland, then the ten children of my grandpar-ents, then the settling nearby of those siblings, and finally each family having children at nearly the same time, so that we could all grow up together. I don't think any of us ever remarked on how unusual it was in America for all this to take place, for the farm to be living through the whole of the twentieth century, and us to be born on it.

We just played and fooled around. As an adolescent, you don't really worry about life or limb, and I doubt I could count all the myriad ways we could have died back then. Reckless as we were, there must have been guardian angels hovering around us the whole time, preventing us from being drowned, shot, blown up, or smashed to pieces in car wrecks. For we cultivated danger, there's no doubt of that—not deliberately, exactly, but just as a matter of course, given the things that interested us. Mainly, we were interested by adrenaline, whose rushes came more readily once we could drive.

Cars gave us distance, and we took it. We used to drive out to Lake Michigan, but it wasn't enough for us to just go to the beach—in fact, we never did that. Instead, we'd go to a bridge that spanned an artificial river flowing from an electric power plant; the water was always warm and fast there. We'd park nearby and then climb out, step by step, hand over hand, to the middle of the bridge, and then drop some thirty feet or more down into the fast-moving green-blue water, fight the current back to shore, climb back up, and jump again. More than once we hung there under the bridge while some plant security man walked above our heads: you could see him moving above us, see his shadow, hear his footsteps. Only years later did my cousin Dan tell me that once when he dived into that water, he hit his forehead on the bottom, and that was the last time he went with us.

When we conceived an idea, we generally went about bringing it into being, and so it was that we decided to buy an old, decrepit pickup truck for bombing around the farm. We searched the papers and found an old truck for sale on the far side of the city; it was sitting in the backyard, rusting, with rounded fenders and a thin, hard steering wheel that turned more than half around before the truck's wheels were affected. For a couple hundred dollars, it was ours, and I remember riding in the passenger seat while Peter Phil drove it across the city at night, a mostly lightless, ancient, clattering, noisy, cold contraption that barely turned a corner at all, and floated down the expressway ballooning across lanes.

What would we do with an old pickup? What else? We drove it to its death, broke it down and broke it up, bouncing and smashing and hooting our way across the fields and trails, just as you'd expect. Conceiving a dislike for a local shopping mall, we seriously discussed the mechanics of disposing of the truck by sending it driverless in one end of the mall and out the other, but alas, it died its second and final death before we could arrange this fiery finale—though we could all envision it hurtling through the glass doors, and making its solitary way through like the juggernaut of progress crashing its way to the light at the other end of the mall tunnel.

Another time, a hapless worker took off for another part of the country and abandoned his car, a subcompact, up at the farm. Eventually someone discovered that he had left the keys, and of course my cousins couldn't resist—you could hear the little four-cylinder engine accelerating down the orchard trails from a quarter mile away, and for a year or two after, there was a shiny chrome bumper roosting in an apple tree on the corner of the trail leading to the storage, other less identifiable rusting parts here and there, perched reminders of how transient machinery is, and how when progress comes to the farm, it often breaks up on the shoals and rocks of restless youth.

In the realm of memory, mainly the uproarious incidents survive. I remember our spirited driving of the old International farm pickup, roaring along the dirt two-tracks to whatever job we were called at the time, and my cousin Dan flying off the back where he had been clinging to the racks, skidding on his stomach into the cucumbers. Or the time we conceived a dislike for a particular street sign and, each time we passed it on our way to the coffee shop, struck it with rotten fruit. Slowly the sign grew blackened and hairy, an unreadable and disgusting pillar of society. Or the arcane art of hitting telephone poles with peaches from a moving truck—a kind of hand-eye coordination that a major league pitcher could envy.

Among all the things we took for granted, probably riding on the back of farm pickups was the most visible to outsiders. Going out to pick sweet corn, we piled on the bushels and clambered on after; going to the coffee shop, we hopped on the back; going out to thin peaches by hand or to cut suckers from the apple trees, we climbed up on the back, and off we'd go down the road. From the truck itself it seemed the most ordinary thing in the world, but I remember my shock when a clerk in a store recognized me and remarked that I was among those guys who rode by on the back of a pickup. Only then did I realize the unusual nature of our transportation, and approach seeing our truck, laden with motley human cargo talking loudly against the wind, the way suburban people must have always seen it—as bizarre.

Riding along on the pickup, shouting into the wind, we came up with some fairly entertaining practical jokes, many of which I don't believe I'll talk about. But there are a couple that will do as well as any to illustrate the rest. One day, years ago, we were out cutting suckers from young Red Delicious trees. Suckers are the young green leafy whips that grow along the inner branches and keep the apples from becoming a deep red; cutting them lets in the sun, and is a usual midsummer job. After a few weeks of sucker-cutting, you begin to lose track of days or time, and the mind naturally turns to diversion. Thus we were delighted, late one morning, to discover that a relative of ours had discarded his old mailbox out in the orchard. It still bore his name, and lay remarkably close to the power-line towers, a circumstance that suggested a natural convergence.

Not too much later, that discarded mailbox had made its way up the gray electric tower some ninety or a hundred feet, and had attached itself, by means of a helpfully supplied old rusty wire, to the center non-electric guy wire that runs along the tip of each tower to the next. The mailbox obligingly moved out and down to the natural dip between towers, where it hung, an oblong scarecrow box in the sky, as out of place as a UFO. It made about as much of a stir as a UFO, too. We were riding to coffee in mid-afternoon when my Uncle Dave noticed the helicopter hovering to the south of the farm. "I wonder what they're over there for?" he asked, his mind undoubtedly on something else. "Hard to say," someone replied.

But it turned out that Consumers Power Company was not terribly amused by the levitating mailbox, and they had a devil of a time getting it off that center guy line, where it hung for some days, an enigmatic speck in the southern sky: you could see the box hanging there even from the road as you drove by, a gratifying sight. The highlight, though, was discovering much later that Consumers Power had used photos of this very mailbox in their videos for schoolchildren, so that every schoolchild in Michigan warned about the dangers of power lines got a close up shot of our relative's mailbox hanging in midair above our orchard. Someone had even put the flag up, so they say. Must have been those thugly neighbor kids.

Yet all such tomfoolery represents only brief moments of uproarious laughter amid hours and days and months and years of hard work, cutting suckers, picking up stones from the fields, picking sweet corn by hand, picking peaches and apples, spreading straw on the strawberries, the endless cycle of seasonal labors. It is common nowadays to lament the plight of immigrant farmworkers, yet farming families that I know themselves work far harder than anyone else, unrelentingly except perhaps for an occasional practical joke, a moment of laughter as we lean against a tree or a truck until we go back to work again.

Our language was often exuberant too. When you're halfway up a full-size McIntosh tree, your feet against its crotch and your back leaning against its largest limb, in your hand a pruning saw, above you the blue summer sky, you sometimes come up with new words, like WITCHET. A witchet stick is a long straight apple whip, on the end of which is placed a small green apple that, when flung into the air, flies like a bullet with a whirring sound. Getting hit by a witchet stick apple is no laughing matter, but mostly we fired them up into the sky to see if we could put one in orbit, or perhaps over the roof of the nearest house.

Sometimes we'd have peach wars, too, hurling small green peaches at one another as we thinned them by hand, until thinning became all-out conflagration, full of ducking, bobbing, and firing among the hanging thin green peach leaves and brittle limbs. Once, I recall, my cousin Peter Joe hit Dan in the head with a pear, and Dan fell down as though mortally wounded, lying unconscious in the grass. We ran up, shocked that he had actually been knocked out, only to see a smile twitch at the corner of his mouth. Dan was good at that kind of thing.

It's strange to look back on what we did in our wild time: it's as though it wasn't really us, and in a sense of course that's true, for as the years go by we become different people, transforming like a stream that passes through different country and that changes with the seasons. There is continuity, but we're not the same. Certainly circumstance was part of it: it took all of us together—or at least a critical mass—to achieve this sort of foolishness, but after all, that's how it is in society as a whole, is it not? One man alone can't ruin an entire continent: it takes countless people, a kind of critical mass, and then people will do things they otherwise couldn't or wouldn't, whether it's to strip mine half a county, or start a war.

There's something strikingly American in the adolescence I'm recounting here; I don't think that should be overlooked. We lived in a world unbounded by consequences, and could do as we willed seemingly without retribution. I think this came in part from the fact that we belonged to the generation born into the age of progress, the middle of the twentieth century, when America was rich and powerful, when all the after effects of the American way of life had yet to come home to roost, before pollution or social decay had become recognized daily realities. There was an illusory quality to American life in that time, the era of suburban homes, of V-8 automobiles (ours was a large green Pontiac with rounded fenders that we called the Dinosaur), of milk trucked to your door every morning. Every family a kingdom, each of us like gods.

How much a boy can take for granted! My cousins and I went to school in a suburban district across the river, and we had nothing in common with those who lived there—we came from across the river, tantamount to being from the Siberian forest. On their side of the river: shabby little stores in rows, house after house side by side for miles, little square suburban yards; on our side of the river: rolling woods and ravines, farms and scattered houses, gravel pits and sand mines. Ours was a different world, and only now do I appreciate the difference, the unboundedness of it, our orchards and fields and horses and dogs, our wild animals and woods. We were initiated into a realm that those people didn't know existed.

We worked, that's for certain, but in another sense we were protected or insulated by the land itself and by our families—not deliberately sheltered, just insulated by the way things were. Sometimes I would imagine what it would be like were the rest of society to collapse and all order vanish—not an outrageous fantasy, I think—and contemplate how we would protect our orchards and fields like some neo-feudal principality. I often thought, and still think today, that if electricity or fuel were unavailable, our fragile social order would soon vanish and we would be fending off the hordes from the nearby city and suburbs. Such a fantasy reveals a fundamental truth about our land: it is a world apart, and belongs to a different order.

Still, in our youth, speculation or contemplation played a singularly small role; we simply lived, carefree. Our family had never seen a divorce; as I noted earlier, our reunions are huge: gathered along aligned picnic tables we fill row after row. We were children living under the shade of a great tree generations old, inheritors of our ancestors' thrift and labor. Only retrospection reveals how rare such a situation is, for one cannot live carefree and at the same time consciously recognize such things; one simply lives, like a tree or a bird. In this sense, consciousness itself means emerging from the Garden, to which there is no reentry save by passing the flaming sword. We were assuming the yoke of commitment that, unbeknownst to us then, our parents bore.

I have talked to others who grew up on family farms, and often they remember tales very much along the lines of those I've told here. Perhaps there's a correlation between the responsibility of owning farmland, of keeping a dozen crops coming along to harvest, and the occasional tomfoolery of youth. But the levity of youth gives way inevitably to the pragmatic world of adulthood, to the era of bills and crying children, of zoning fights and taxes. Indeed, the day might come when one looks back on youthful escapades and wishes they had not happened, depending on how hidebound one has become. For seen on balance, youthful exuberance always has in it a darkness, a callousness to others. That's just how it is.

But would I exchange such stories for a sanitized ordinary suburban life? Would I relinquish all these memories for a pocketful of silver? Of course not. To live fully means that you embrace everything, bring it all into the light of consciousness—darkness and suffering, joy and exuberance. It's no good trying to sanctimoniously reject all the "bad things" and cling to only what we now perceive as good. That way, you end up dry and dusty, mouthing platitudes, as empty as a brown cornhusk. Lifejuice comes from having roots deep in the dirt: a plant can't reject the dirt and live. Those who are fully alive accept the whole of life; they don't cling to anything but enjoy everything.

When we were children, we spoke as children and did childish things; but when we became men we put away the things of childhood. So it always is. There is a continuity between the "I" of those days, and this "I" who writes these words—but between the two is an unfathomable gulf, and I do not think the one would at all have expected the other, this one who sits here now, writing. I have been around the world more than once, have lived through all manner of adventures, hobnobbed with all sorts of people, and have slowly become someone else, transformed from the inside out. Some believe that we are genetically or environmentally determined, but this isn't so: who we are changes through time, emerges in time's tapestry, is woven by our intentions and experiences and actions.

What remains of all that we have done? There are two ways we remain: written in consciousness, and written in the earth. These are our traces, and why the farm is itself a tribute to transgenerational duty and reverence. We remember these silly exploits, but nothing remains of them except our memories—and during the same time, we were all learning, day by day, how the earth slopes in a certain place, how it feels to hoe a field all day, what it's like to sucker an orchard, or to thin twenty acres of peaches. These are the activities that left their mark, cumulatively, in the earth itself, and though there is little trace of any particular hoeing or trimming or thinning, still there is a cumulative effect both in the mind and on the land.

America is the land of perpetual adolescence: our youthful hijinks mirror those of the whole society, careless and callous and laughing at consequences, always ready to move on to new territory, fearless and full of good humor, rarely thinking about the way things are but just accepting circumstance. And yet there is within our clan an Old World insularity, the protection of the family, and this is not so characteristically American, for America is the land of the loner, too, of separation, isolation. Perhaps, in this new world, it is not surprising that my cousins and I each went our separate ways, moved on into the outside world and mostly disappeared from one another's view, so that later it was almost as if we had never known one another. Only the land remained in common, and only we who still worked on it remained in touch. One day, to our surprise, we discovered that we had grown up.

# Characters Quick or Dead

A grizzled brown face, deep lines in his forehead, a perpetual squint, gray stubble, a hook nose with wide nostrils, a brown formal fur felt hat, its brim ribbon stained with sweat, and a long, foul tan raincoat that he wore even if it was a hundred degrees outside. He'd climb onto the back of the truck, and rope one arm along the rack, his big-knuckled brown hand holding the top of the wooden strut, his other hand down at his side, ride along with the wind whipping his coat and woolen pants, gazing ahead fiercely, sometimes staring into the sun. He had a unique, instantly recognizable voice that would intone, nasally, "O by gol." His name was Mark Baer, and not a one of us has forgotten him, though he died years ago. Like so many of the workers who've come and gone on the farm, he was truly a character.

Long gone, and yet he lives on in our memories of him: my cousin Dan can probably still mimic his voice, and one summer mimicked Mark Baer so well that my uncle worked himself into a near lather out in the peaches. He'd call "Basket, Mark!" and in the distance, beyond the green tropical thin leaves of the outermost row, he'd hear the mumbling of Mark's voice: "O yes, basket—over to the south, by gol, south by southwest, yes sir. Had heifer eyes, that girl. O by gol."

"Basket!"

"Over to the south, yes, might rain in a day or two, O by gol."

You get the picture: it went on like that while those who had figured out what was going on were collapsing with laughter along with Dan over by the pickup; he'd emerge from convulsive laughing long enough to offer yet another perfect imitation of Mark Baer, who wasn't there at all that day.

It's curious how many of these characters have worked on the farm over the years, and how remarkably clear our memory of them is. It's not that we just reminisce about them on occasion—people can actually mimic them, their characteristic exchanges, the striking way they'd talk. There are people I can remember—whose mannerisms and peculiar speech patterns I know perfectly—and I've never actually met them at all. Memories of them are carried on in passing conversations among older men while we're shaking straw with forks, covering the strawberry plants before winter sets in; or again, when we're hoeing, or maybe out in the orchard. Iggy, Big Ed, Mark Baer, Doc, Jack Dawsey: there's a kind of resurrection by remembering, and one wonders anew about the uniqueness of each individual. It survives, as the ancient poet Homer would say, by the singer's memory.

You ought to know, I guess, that these fellows lived on the edge, mostly. Some turned up in town stabbed to death, others shot, or dead from alcohol—and sometimes they disappeared, never traveling in with the others in the spring, just vanishing. "You heard from Jack?" somebody would ask, and someone would say "I heard he died in Florida," or something of the sort. Maybe he did, maybe not. Sometimes, like a ghost, a fellow would return quietly to the farm after a decade gone, surprisingly there one morning as the light turned pale and bright, as if for him it was the day that the grave-sleepers awake.

That happened once with Jack Dawsey, who one day after more than a decade was back as if he had never left, sitting on the gray boulder just past the corner of the white tool shed, his bony hands resting on his knees. His face was brown and lined, his black hair combed back and glistening a little, but he moved slower and more awkwardly than he once did, and you could see the thinness of his legs and arms through his clothes when he walked. For a long time he lived somewhere nearby, almost outdoors, and when you walked past you could sometimes smell something frying on a little stove. Nobody told him to leave, or complained about him; he was mostly left alone, and he helped out when there was something to do. He had come back to die. Eventually he did, in a hospital, and his sister came to see him first. "He'd never take help," she said, in a resigned voice, the voice of someone who knew the incorrigible.

What is it that drives these fellows to live their lives on the edge of society? I imagine that somewhere right now there's a clustering group of white-coated technoids who are trying to isolate the gene that causes a man to become a Mark Baer, a Jack Dawsey, that pulls him away from the ordinary routines of life and toward alcohol and the bad part of town, toward bar fights and prostitutes, cross-country jaunts in an illegal, barely running car. But it's not so hard to see how, as our machine-society accelerates, clattering and tacking on new parts at an ever more furious pace, some people refuse to be a part of it. These folks who don't fit into our consumerist machine very well might have an intensity of personality that many perfectly functional drones have long since relinquished. They might even be more deeply human than many who sit in judgment of them in their air-conditioned offices.

I'm not romanticizing the hobo here. There's nothing romantic about being at the bottom of American society, about getting stabbed on a foul, dim-lit street and staggering over to lean against a decaying brick wall while bits of discarded colored paper and plastic blow past you or lodge against you. Nothing romantic about lifting a heavy wooden ladder in the bright morning cold with aching hands, head throbbing from the whiskey of the night before, which you hardly remember. Nothing romantic about dying alone, of cirrhosis or cancer, your body eaten away from the inside. Nothing romantic about these things at all.

And yet. And yet I think it's far too easy for those of us who wish to live in a glossy catalogue world to pretend that these people don't exist, or to try and legislate them away—to ignore who they are and what they really mean. Because they do have meaning—they are meaningful. Each one of them we remember with absolute clarity, testament to the enduring significance, the delight one takes in the human personality, even in the surly, deceitful, arrogant, and stupid, not to mention the witty, the crafty, the quick-fingered, and those who somehow became almost self-caricatures, having laid the tracks of their behavior so that now their personalities ride like empty cars along its rails. Still, the world is richer for them, every one, lying or honest, quick or dead.

And quick or dead is about the right phrase here. For these fellows, the line between life and death is clearly drawn, and they know perhaps more than many of us what a dead man looks like. There's Casey, for instance, who's been reported dead on numerous occasions, only to reappear unexpectedly the next season. Casey is—or was, assuming he's really dead, a dubious assumption, given his history—a small, thin, wiry, hyperactive man with white hair, flashing gimlet eyes, and a dangerously loud mouth. It's little wonder he's been in the hospital repeatedly, stabbed or nearly beaten to death; he's rather like a banty rooster that doesn't know when to quit, and pipes up even when he's close to being shot. I asked him once about being in the hospital, and he said it wasn't bad—just give them some name, and they'll take you in. "Good food," he added with a grin.

The thing about men like Casey is, they don't die easily. They're hardened; they can take what would probably kill you or me, and still show up the next morning to lug corn or pick peaches. The 1950s longshoreman-philosopher Eric Hoffer held that America's real life is lived by these kinds of people, not by the wealthy or aristocratic, but by the folks who work with their hands, those who need another start, those who are down and out, as the expression has it. And he's right, I think. These people are closer to the raw sources of life; they do live on the edge. I once (just for conversation) asked a tall, sunburned man with no front teeth, who went by the name of Doc, about his driver's license. "Driver's license?" he said, incredulous. Surely I wasn't foolish enough to think that he'd go into some official place and fill out some form. But he drove a battered car, I ventured. "All the way across the country," he replied. What did he do when he was pulled over by a policeman? "They cain't keep you in jail forever, now, can they?" He smiled a toothless happy grin.

Sometimes we have women workers, too. There's Ginny, for instance, who comes to pick blueberries when they're ripe and she's so inclined. She walks up the road with furious determination on her sharp face, her clothes mismatched and loose, her mousy-brown hair all askew, stalks into the barn, picks up a clattering tin pail, and heads down to the blueberries. If you talk to her, she'll shout back, sometimes, and you'll know within a couple of words that you're dealing with someone like Mark Baer—who's not, as they say, all there. Her voice sounds like it's filtered strangely. Sometimes she'll get enraged over nothing, and other times she'll be fairly happy, but you'll never really know why in either case. She picks her blueberries well enough, if slowly, and in a few hours, she'll have filled a couple of pails. When you pay her, she'll stamp off just the way she came.

And then there's Sue and John, who drive in from down south in their battered copper-colored pickup, sleeping in the back or outside, along with their boy, now a gangly quiet adolescent. Sue is a large woman, her legs each as big around as a half bushel, and she breathes hard sometimes when she picks fruit, but she works right alongside the others, rarely talking and never breaking stride for anything. John, on the other hand, red-haired, florid, mustachioed and tattooed, is voluble, and talks with a marble-mouthed Southern accent that's almost incomprehensible, words strung together like beads flitting by, and you can glimpse the color of some but not all. "Caintletawomangetoneoveronye," he'll say, but you know all too well that when it comes down to shoving, Sue wins.

How do these people find their way to us? Perhaps it is partly the longevity of the place itself—the land is always there, and open to them for work. It's a place where these outsiders can come and go freely; they're treated just like anyone else, and they make a little money. But perhaps too they're complementary to the clean, orderly piety of our Dutch Calvinist family—maybe they're the wild side of our conservatism. Certainly they're necessary—without them, it would be impossible to harvest acres of fruit and vegetables, so there's definitely a symbiosis between asocial rogues and our relentlessly conservative attitude toward work and life. We need each other: they need us to come to; we need them to come to us, making meandering pilgrimages from farm to farm across America, while we stay here, up every morning at dawn.

I imagine that Jacobus James Versluis worked with characters like this too. There were probably more of them in his day, in fact. For the more bureaucratically regulated society becomes, the harder it is to continue. Undoubtedly in the old days, James probably paid people off from a small wad of cash; my guess is he never kept books. Money came in, money went out, with few intermediaries. But nowadays, there are a thousand regulations: there are ladder rules and insurance regulations, workman's compensation laws, tax laws, and all kinds of idiot legislation with destructive effects, whatever the intentions behind it. All of this gets in the way of the obvious, simple, necessities of life, and might even drive out some characters, along with more than a few farmers.

I'll give you an example. When I was growing up, we picked strawberries—and so did children from all over the neighborhood, especially from our extended family. We had some acres of straw-berries, some wooden crates and quarts, and with my Uncle Warren and Jim Van Dyken supervising, we kids would all line up along the green-leaf rows, kneel down on the golden straw, and pick. Admittedly, nobody got rich doing this—not the farm nor the children—but mothers were relieved of their children for the morning of a summer's day, and children learned about hard work and what money meant. It's one thing, after all, to buy a bicycle with money you've been given, and quite another to pick straw-berries for it at a nickel or dime a quart. No question: do that, and you'll look at money differently the rest of your life.

And it's an education for people to pick berries, too. Every pos-sibility was realized at one time or another: there were berry fights, and crushed berries in quarts, rocks in quarts, straw in quarts (with a topping of berries), green berries, wailing two-year-olds and pugnacious towhead bullies, berry field seductions or flirtations, berry-picking races, kids running across the field heedlessly, thun-derstorms, tornado warnings and sirens blaring while the sky turned green-yellow, lightning bolts shattering a tree down in the swamp, straw that caught fire, kids who walked home after half an hour or half a morning, feuding parents, loquacious grandparents, and who knows what else? Every day had its minor dramas, most of them amusing.

But then came legislation to "protect" children and garner tax money. For along came the requirement that the farm file individ-ual tax and Social Security accounts for every one of those chil-dren. Think about that. You get some children who will come for one day—still have to file that four dollars and twenty cents. Now this is just exactly the kind of idiocy you'd expect from the federal and state governments, because of course what it means is that we cannot have children pick strawberries anymore. Who could han-dle that kind of paperwork? And why would anyone want to? Because you know perfectly well that the penalties for infractions would be onerous—we'd probably all be in jail. You'd have to build a couple extra prisons to house us all.

So there's no more children picking berries, and the connections between the farm and the neighborhood are the poorer for it. I still meet people who say, in passing, "I remember working on your family's farm picking strawberries when I was a kid. Remember it clearly. . ." And then they'll describe my uncle, and a field, and much else with great detail, often with a kind of wistfulness. Children, you see, grow up; and grown up, they remember what it was like to actually pick strawberries. Strawberries in the grocery store have a different meaning for them; they know that berries don't just mysteriously appear, plastic-covered, in some replicator-machine, but rather are picked by someone bent over and laboring. What's more, they even know the local farm, remember it as a child remembers it. The farm means something to them, too. Some of those children were characters, but by working in the strawberries, we all gained character as well.

It's a precious thing, this farm. It's not just land; it's a whole economy in the broadest sense of the word, a link between all kinds of people, and many of them you'd not expect if you weren't connected with it. There's a former pesticide salesman who'd come driving up in his pickup and invariably rest his arm on his pickup window and say to someone, while we were trimming trees or picking or something, "Where's. . . Dave?" He luxuriated in pauses, and some of the guys like to joke that he . . . was . . . a . . . little . . . slow. But the truth is, he was a good fellow, and even if he wasn't, he was a *character*. The farm generates characters; you might even say it generates character, although I wouldn't insist on the point.

For that matter, my mother is something of a character: when the local Road Commission decided one day that it would cut down all the huge elderly maples alongside the nearby highway, she grew incensed and, after some drone bureaucrat told her that those trees were all an impediment to progress, she was furious. Not content with just a telephone call, she organized some neighbors and some picketing, got herself on the evening news, and finally the Road Commission, realizing what it was up against, decided to leave the trees alone. There is something satisfying in being able to win such a battle, even if it is only a temporary victory, and it takes a character to do so.

I can't leave this theme without mentioning my Uncle Rob. Technically he's not my uncle; his father was my grandfather Peter's brother Paul. Originally, Peter and Paul owned houses across from one another on top of the hill, and farmed together, but Paul died in 1955, and no one in his family kept farming. Paul's original house was sold, but Rob and his wife built a small house on a cul-de-sac just below it. Rob was the prototypical curmudgeon; he was also amusingly witty. He had some circulation problems in his legs, and so walked stiffly with short steps; he had a sunburned face and thinning dark hair combed back. Undoubtedly he couldn't have gotten along without his wife, Clara, a kindly gray-haired woman who finished his sentences for him.

Rob delivered his morose, sardonic observations on the world without a smile, and some of his observations are legendary in the family. To say that Rob was a curmudgeon is only to say the obvious, and yet he was a good-hearted curmudgeon. Once at the coffee shop he and Clara were sitting near us, and Rob told the story of how an acquaintance of his had been eating in a restaurant recently, and had slumped face forward into his soup, dead from heart failure. We waited. "What a way to go," Rob said appreciatively, without a hint of a smile, though you could see in his eyes that the idea was attractive to him. "What a way to go."

Rob often helped us on the farm by collecting money from the visitors who came to pick their own blueberries or strawberries. Mostly he could sit in peace with his cronies, morose men in their sixties or seventies like himself, some of whom were laconic at best; they would share silence, poker, and sour observations. But occasionally Rob was extremely busy, with dozens of people to supervise including boisterous children whom he regarded with a jaundiced eye in the manner of W. C. Fields. He had seen everything, he once told me while sitting on his rusted metal chair outside the red blueberry shack. "You can't believe what stupid things people will do," he said. "Leave their berries in the field in pails and drive away; fall into the swamp water; pick on the opposite side from where I tell them; try to sneak off without paying; try to leave their kids here. There's no end to it." He paused, looked out over the blueberry plants toward the horizon. "People." He sighed. "I'm glad I'm not one of them." Rob died not long ago, but his character lives on.

For it seems to me that being a character includes having character—they're facets of the same thing, in the end. The godlike Odysseus would lie when it suited the situation, but he wasn't a liar; he was a character, so much so that the goddess Athena herself would keep an eye out for him. The gods and goddesses recognized a major character when they saw one, and they reacted accordingly, not necessarily with a reward, but always with appreciation, with recognition that this was someone unique, remarkable, even if their recognition entailed throwing him off course or trying to kill him. And there's a sense in which we all react like this: we may delight in or despise a character, but either way, we respect one when we see one, even if it's only in our heart, unexpressed.

The more one comes to understand the inexpressible mystery out of which life's profusion emerges, as out of Lao Tsu's mysterious valley, the more extraordinary and precious is each of these characters. Perhaps they are so precious precisely because they are transient, because we know they might not return for another year, that indeed, everything is transient, delicately balanced and always in flux. And seen in memory's golden light, all these people and the place itself, the land's lineaments, glow. Poetry, tinged with sadness, expresses this mysterious appreciation, this love of the fleeting, and perhaps all literature worthy of the name consists in efforts to embody this love of the particular, of the unique, of characters and of a land's character.

# The Wild Ones

Here on the farm you'll see them sometimes at dusk or at dawn, silent, poised, round tan bodies on delicate legs, heads turned toward you, brown eyes gazing. They are like spirits floating over sharp hooves, ghostlike in the morning mist or twilight. If you freeze, they might turn, walk on their way, but more often they'll bolt, and like gazelles, bound among the trees and disappear from view. One might pause, though, and look back at you, just to see what you're doing, and perhaps your eyes will meet, in that moment some mysterious communication taking place. That's the point at which worlds join, natural and human, over the brown tall grass of Island Farm.

You might think that a farm is wholly domesticated, but that's not so. In fact, it's an enclave for wild ones, especially the woods and the puckerbrush, where all manner of creatures are. Of course, they're mostly shy of humans, and for good reason. The roar of a tractor or a chain saw, the blast of a shotgun or a rifle, are not calculated to lure in those whose natural lair draws a shroud of silence around itself. But under those brown and tangled grasses lurk mice and shrews, while above them circle red-tailed hawks, wings outstretched and eyes keening; in the shrubbery might be a raccoon or a gray opossum like some mutant overgrown rat; and in the trees red or fox squirrels leap lightly from limb to limb.

How rarely we think about these creatures, though they are always there, as long as the land allows it. I've so many times been struck by how isolated are the suburbanites whose houses surround our farm. On a brilliantly blue autumn day, you can walk for miles, and although you'll see house after house, even apartments, you might well never see a single man, woman, or child outside. They're almost certainly watching some flickering screen, absorbed in images of the outside world in the weird rituals of substitution and deception that pass for entertainment. Most people nowadays, I think, live inside and seldom venture out, almost as if the surrounding world were some kind of jungle. And the fact is, it might as well be a jungle to them.

My cousins Peter Joseph and Nathan have, every now and then, broached the possibility of setting loose wild hogs on the farm, and I have to admit, there's something appealing about the notion. As it is, visitors often seem to think that when they're venturing into the blueberry patch it might as well be a Vietnamese jungle, as though to go out into an orchard or an open, untilled field is roughly equivalent to entering the Amazon. But that's probably not so farfetched, given the antiseptic, coldly lit, air-conditioned sterility of the average suburban dweller's home, work place, and market. If you had wild hogs, people would really have to be on their guard when they went to pick their own blueberries. They'd never know when some tusky, ugly herd of boars and sows would come squealing around the next bush and run down their fat, drowsy toddler or poodle.

There's not enough sense of respect for wild creatures anymore. Most people live isolated from the animals' world; they become shining eyes glimpsed briefly as we drive by; they lie, humped, small, delicate, alongside the road as if asleep; they are unknown, unseen. It is curious, when you think about it, how much the human world now is engineered to wholly exclude the wild ones. Oh, it's true that a pair of hawks might spiral on updrafts high over your suburban tract—but you won't see them, nor will they see you, ensconced as you are in your sealed dwelling, or walking briskly to your sealed vehicle whose door will close with a satisfyingly metallic solidity. Perhaps we moderns need a hawk to drop down and lift off with a child or a cat, just to remind us that there are wild ones in this world still.

But we don't have wild boars or child-snatching hawks where I'm from, and most wildlife has to run like deer. Deer, you see, hide. They know where the swamplands and the woodlands are; they take refuge in the deep ravines or the long woods on the highlands along the river, or nearer the farm, where there are enough trees for cover and foraging. We see them, sometimes, between the rows of apple trees, like tan apparitions, floating dreamlike as they bound away. Sometimes we surprise them on their journeys from one safe place to another, on their longer peregrinations, far more dangerous nowadays, given the speed of vehicles and the likelihood of being shot.

It's revealing, I think, that the deer is such a harmless creature for most people, and yet so relentlessly hunted. For an apple farmer, deer today are a curse, of course—they nibble the green shoots of newly planted trees, and left unchecked can destroy a whole young orchard. Many's the times we've hung bars of soap or bags of dried blood in the trees, hoping to forestall their destructiveness. My uncle claims that deer are just large rats, and his antipathy is well founded. But they pose no threat to the suburbanites who, year after year, drive around with spotlights, poaching deer by temporarily blinding them and then shooting them; who nail large unsightly platforms in the little woods that still remain; who seem willing to do almost anything to "bag a deer."

Countless times I've been out walking my dog, or just walking, and have come across a hastily hacked up carcass and pile of red-white entrails. There's a kind of deer-hunting subculture in America, and it isn't anything like what you read about in glossy magazines. Its tenor is perhaps best captured in the ubiquitous signs come autumn, in gas stations and corner stores, advertising "Beer and Ammunition." Its results are perhaps best suggested by the staggering, pain-crazed, gutshot doe that lay, bleeding and shaking, in the orchard the other day. From its back and side protruded several target arrows, now festering and smelling rancid. These aren't pretty images, but they're true, and they help explain why deer run when they see people.

One day I was coming home from what was then Graham Agricultural Experiment Farm across the four-lane highway, when the first doe burst through the swamp underbrush behind the houses to the south and, without hesitating, bounded between cars going fifty miles an hour. Behind her came another, then another, until seven deer were crossing that highway, in a frenzy to escape someone undoubtedly crashing through the swamp on the far side. The deer, I think, knew the highway's danger, but they knew too that one might cross the highway safely, so they ran. Cars and trucks stopped, ceasing their own frenzied rushing for these animals, parting what could be a Red Sea, just for a moment. I held my breath. And the last deer was wounded—she couldn't quite leap the page-wire fence, but, pathetically, terror-stricken, scrabbled and thrashed before it. Her herd paused among the apple trees, looked back—and then, miraculously, she was over and gone.

Perhaps what we do to deer is a measure of who, or what, we are. And maybe that moment when traffic paused to let those terrified does bound past, maybe that was a sign of human nature as it can be, willing for an instant to let wild ones be. But I'm inclined to think, Calvinist in my bones, that the only reason no one gutshot those deer on the spot is that no one had a rifle handy. Total depravity is as good an explanation as any for why people so relentlessly hunt these creatures, year round, day and night, with rifles and arrows. It's one thing to run a deer down on foot and kill it with your bare hands, as some tribes are reputed to have enjoined their young men to do; it's quite another to gutshoot a doe from an illegal permanent tree stand after you put food out for her.

If such are the means by which our society is to be measured, it has some ways to go before civilization. Perhaps missionaries from an actual culture could come and teach the rudiments. Machinery and convenience are too often mistaken for civilization nowadays, but in fact civilization can be measured only by whether we live in harmony with nature, with one another, and with the divine. This harmony comes about through kindness. We know intuitively what is right, I think, and no heap of arguments about deer herd population or anything else will change the feeling one has upon seeing a pain-crazed, dying wild animal, whose only crime was to live too near humans.

All this doesn't change the fact, however, that for the apple farmer, the deer are a pestilence. I know a farmer who went so far as to put up a high electric fence around his entire orchard so that it resembles a prison yard, but of course the deer do make their way over it, just as he knew they would. Yet the main problem is not the deer population, but the human. People keep building houses in the woods, along the woods, paving over the deer's natural lairs, filling up swamps with cement, and so, year by year, the deer are forced into larger herds, roaming in a land increasingly alien to them that is populated by hostiles. Against these new and larger herds, the beleaguered farmer hangs his talismans of dried blood and soap, and sometimes this even seems to work.

But in a way, I think that the deer and the farm are in a similar plight. The deer take refuge in the few remaining stands of deep woods and marshes, increasingly even among the apple trees, which themselves are endangered by a society not only indifferent to farming, but even, alas, often hostile to its values. I suppose it is not too much to ask that one be left alone to be what one is— yet our society seems unable to leave either the deer or the farm alone. The same indifference that characterizes also characterizes the trespasser driving over our young apple saplings with a snowmobile, the poacher shining deer, and the so-called developer whose shortsighted profit-seeking culminates in destroying the land upon which both deer and apples can live.

For land can be gutshot too, you see. In fact, that's how I'd characterize the parking lots, apartment complexes, strip malls, and subdivisions from which rainwater rushes, draining onto our land, flooding our fields. Ah, you say, but that's "progress." It's "inevitable." And even if it's not, we affirm the right of the individual to do anything he damn well pleases with the land he owns, don't we? Indeed, more than that, we encourage its sale for paving and "improvement," while enacting utterly self-destructive trade legislation that makes it impossible for the farmer to make a profit by selling his crops locally—for he's undercut by someone in equally desperate straits in some far-off country whose land is also endangered, and who's sold his crop to some middleman at a loss. And so we gutshoot the world, and call it progress.

When you think about it, every creature just wants to live unbothered. That's true of the red-tailed hawk, and of the thin-striped garter snake, its prey; of the vole and the woodchuck, of the sparrow and the raccoon, of the squirrel and the owl. One can find all these animals out in the fields, orchards, or woods at twilight, and all of them, like the land itself, seek just to be themselves. Only human beings prevent them, and I often wonder how we must appear to them with our roaring machinery and indiscriminate slaughtering, our sterile paved flatlands; surely it must seem like some incomprehensible invasion, and one can only speculate what animals in council might say to one another, gathered in some blue-lit grove at midnight.

However fanciful such a scene might seem, it is, I think, closer to reality than the bizarre contemporary belief that human beings and animals are wholly separate, that animals are like biomechanisms in whose survival we may have some interest, but from whom we are ineluctably distant. Some American Indian tribes held that animal spirits did meet in council, and that they would discuss such things as human behavior. Surely if ever human behavior merited comment from such an outsider's perspective, now is the time, for we have certainly made them outsiders. How do we recover an awareness of the fundamental links between humans, animals, and the divine? Perhaps we need totems, manifested recognition that these three are ultimately one, for even if today those totems are seen merely in the distorted mascots of sports teams, still the possibility exists, and it may be that only thus can we awaken again to what wild ones mean. Fur and feathers of the soul. *Anima mundi.*

Walking along a ridge one sunny day in the late winter, I happened upon a hawk, one of three who lived and hunted over our land—parents and a child. A fluttering sound, great tan-brown wings against the bare tree limbs, feathers rustling against bark as the hawk rose up from among the gray trunks, bearing in its talons a writhing serpent. At first I did not recognize it, only knew to look that way, and then those wings and that body, that curved beak and those eyes, the hanging talons, all took form as if the earth and trees had suddenly given birth to it before my startled gaze. And then the wide wings were spread: the great bird was free of those trees' outstretched limbs and rose up, up into the vast and cloudless sky.

A hawk disdains the earthbound. Soaring above every other creature, a hawk gazes with a cruel and precise serenity, and its raw distant cry bespeaks wildness everywhere it is heard. Often you will see one or even two of them perched upon the highest metal struts of the power-line towers bisecting our farm, perhaps on the hill overlooking the blueberries. Were you to climb the tower, and get to the highest point, you'd hear the crackling of the electricity for the whole city passing around you, and spread out around you would be the whole farm and all the surrounding countryside, even unto the apartments, condominiums, strip malls, and highway. From here the hawk would spread its wings and soar, circling on currents, keening for its prey.

Sauntering along an orchard trail, enjoying a perfect ease, I have seen a hawk, or even two or three, spiraling high above the farm as if they are its eternal guardians. The favored totem of the Pennsylvania Dutch was the double eagle with outstretched wings, and I have a renewed appreciation for why this was so, having watched so many hawks, graceful sky dancers. An image like this inspires one with an inarticulate longing and, paradoxically, with a freedom from worldly human concerns, as if to see a hawk is in itself to be reminded not of military power, but of spiritual freedom, which is, after all, the only freedom. Sometimes when I was far from the farm, as I traveled back I would see hawks alongside the road or in the air, as if they were guiding me home.

And one day, while out under the turquoise sky-sea, I glimpsed a hawk high above the city that was sprawling out in its noisy chaos beneath us, and—I hesitate to write this, lest I be misunderstood—we were for a time one, the hawk soaring above, and I standing on the ridge below, united by an inexpressible and inviolable joy in simply being, a love, not of any one thing but of every particular thing. What can be said of such a moment? Perhaps the time was or will come when this might be not a rare instant, but now it is. Indeed, perhaps it's only when this is so that we have started to understand what it means to be human, defined ultimately not by what we have exploited or manipulated but by who we are, and where.

# Farm Dogs

Every farm boy ought to have a dog to walk and play with. But having a dog is a singular occupation; I know a rancher who has eighteen dogs, and though I admire him for his love of the animals, that's not what I'm talking about. Entering his yard, you're surrounded by dogs—German shepherds and Australian shepherds, a lumbering sheep-guarding dog and a hound, a sleek and skulking part-Doberman, and numerous Border collies. Yet a surfeit of dogs is not what I needed as a boy; I needed a single dog, one that knew me and the land, and what a dog ought to do, a dog with pride, perhaps even a dog that believed it was human.

When I was fourteen, my mother and I went down to the local humane society and walked among the sad, frightened, caged creatures that gazed forlornly out through the wire mesh. There were huskies and shepherds and dachshunds, but when I saw the small masked puppies, that's where my attention fixed. I stood and watched them, especially a little white one with black markings, including a black mask over her ears and eyes. She was different from the others—not insouciant, but still, she had a presence even there among her siblings, who crawled about and whimpered. I didn't have any doubt—this was the pup I would take home.

I remember going for walks through deep snow, and behind me she'd leap and sink, or trot along the path I'd made. Sometimes the snow was drifted chest high, so that from a distance you'd see only a head seeming to float orphically above the white, and you'd see no pup at all. Nothing much seems to be going on during such peregrinations, but all the same, something happens on the inside. You and the dog are walking together in some inner landscape, too.

I had chosen, of course, the smartest dog that had ever lived. We didn't know this at first: puppies bound about, cavort, grip onto a proffered sock and growl, but you can't really tell what manner of dog it is that you have on the other end of the sock. Oh, some say that you can tell, and I suppose there were signs, but she did nothing spectacular as a pup—no spontaneous Mozart recitals, in any event. She was a Border collie mix, although at that time I had never even heard of a Border collie, and didn't know that they were renowned for their intelligence. Intelligence in a dog might sound desirable, but you have to be aware that a dog can have too many smarts for its own good, and that was certainly the case with Bonnie. She had her own views on all sorts of things, chiefly when she deemed it the right time to go for a long foray through the vicinity, but also when she wanted to get out of the house or out of a room. You couldn't keep her in if she got her mind set on going somewhere else.

I'm told that there are two kinds of working Border collies: those whose every movement is controlled by the master, and those that just go off and do what needs to be done. Bonnie was the latter, in spades. She'd go off and do what she conceived needed doing, oftentimes something that humans found didn't need doing at all. But that didn't stop her, not in the least. For instance, she would occasionally come trotting proudly into the yard, bearing some silken gift, someone's underwear fetched in from a clothesline perhaps half a mile away. And what do you do with someone else's silken underpants? Do you go from house to house, inquiring?

But fetching underwear is a puppy's endeavor, and as she grew to adulthood, she put aside the things of puppyhood, and took upon herself the task of woodchuck killing. In an orchard, one or two woodchucks are not a bad thing, generally—but when they breed and become numerous, inevitably they will unearth the roots of a tree, digging down under the trunk. Then too, a vertical woodchuck hole in the middle of a trail can break a horse's leg, not to mention the occasional bizarre sight of a woodchuck clambering up into a tree's limbs and gnawing at the fruit. Woodchucks are not a pestilence like flocks of grackles, but they sometimes are an irritant.

Their very existence was an irritant to Bonnie. Whereas most dogs would leave woodchucks alone, she saw it as her mission to eradicate them; she memorized the location of their holes. She knew where the main, exposed holes were with their piles of tamped sandy soil, and she knew where the hidden, rear-entrance holes were; she knew how best to stalk a woodchuck that sat up like a prairie dog near its hidden hole, and how to cut it off. When it clacked its teeth and fought, she wasn't intimidated, and sometimes she'd come trotting back home bearing in her jaws a limp gray-brown body so large that she could barely manage it, the sodden corpse heavy as a bag of rocks. Occasionally the woodchuck would scrabble up a tree and she'd catch it halfway up, leaping in the air and dragging it down.

But most remarkable was how she killed them, with a quick shake of her head, breaking their neck with an astonishing suddenness and ferocity. Around people she was an exceedingly sweet dog, what my sisters called a "mush dog," who'd lean against your leg and place her head under your hand. Yet faced with a woodchuck she was unerring and ruthless, the most efficient killer I have ever seen. I was once with her atop the hill near the farmhouse, and she glimpsed something far, far away in the rowed cornfield down below. She ran down the hill, flat out, hit that roaming woodchuck with full force, bowling it end over end, and by the time it might have regained its balance, it was dead in her jaws. You could tell her no, but it just wouldn't matter.

That uncompromising will of hers extended beyond woodchucks, sometimes. There was a dog down the street, a hybrid shepherd, that would run out and chase people who walked by, and once it bit one of my aunts as she walked along the road in the morning. I heard about the incident at the coffee shop, and that evening, I went for a stroll with Bonnie. When we reached that house, where machinery was piled up in the yard, out came the snarling shepherd dog with its teeth bared. It was twice as big as Bonnie, but she didn't hesitate—she went straight for it, and of course it ran. She pursued it onto its own porch, and there commenced quite a ruckus, after which she trotted down the road beside me again, her chest bloody, though there wasn't a scratch on her.

I never encouraged her in any of this, but I didn't dissuade her either—that would have been futile. She was simply doing what she was meant to do, fulfilling what in India would be called her svadharma. It's easy enough, I suppose, for people who live their whole lives viewing animals behind bars or through glass to ignore the cruel certainty with which animals will kill, the truth that suffering pervades the whole of nature. There's a cruel nobility in this, too, though, a pride that can't be overlooked, in the way Bonnie would walk, in the way she'd gaze through brown eyes out on a world whose inhabitants one leaned against, killed, or ignored. It's just how she was.

In the summer we bale hay, and throw the bales onto a trailer pulled by a green John Deere tractor, and I remember one summer when Bonnie was in her prime, we'd stacked a load as high as we could—seven or eight layers—and we were sitting on top of it, someone just getting ready to drive the load home. That's always the best part of haying—riding back on top of a high load. But

Bonnie wanted to come along, and so, just to see what would happen, I called to her from atop that load. She leaped up, caught herself on the first couple of bales and somehow, miraculously, managed to climb all the way to where I sat. To this day I have no idea how she did it—it's roughly like climbing the side of a building bare-handed—but it shows clearly enough her indomitable will, that image of white-haired Bonnie, tail waving, high atop a load of hay going down the road to the barn.

In her day, she was a fine dog, and I retain images of her still: her running alongside the truck down the road, astonishingly fast, past mailboxes and through yards at twenty or twenty-five miles an hour; her finding me out in the middle of a sweet-corn field, winding her way through the jungle of tall green plants, soaking wet and dirty, and gently nudging my leg with her nose to remind me she'd found me; her leaping into the scratched pickup bed and standing, smiling, among us as we rode to the coffee shop; her disappearing for a day or more, only to return exhausted and blackened from who knows what dog's adventures in the far woods; a white blur as she leaped into the air to pull a woodchuck from a tree; her lying beneath the bushes on a summer evening, watching the world with imperious eyes.

People have all sorts of pejorative expressions that feature dogs: a dog's life; she's a dog; it's a dog on the market. And dogs can have miserable lives, no doubt about it. A dog chained up day and night in some white-trash backyard might well be better off dead, and I have heard such a critter lament its lot in life with almost unbearable sorrow. But a dog's life can also be delightful and arguably better than most people's. What a life Bonnie led! Countless acres of open land to roam; care and affection; all sorts of interesting people to sniff; woodchucks to hunt; and a boy to go on walks with or to work on the farm, where she could ride like a queen in the pickup. Some dogs definitely are smarter and have more charming and developed personalities than many people—

and live more interesting lives. I think Bonnie was on her way to becoming human; certainly she thought so.

There were more than a few miracles in her life. She was hit at least twice by cars, once so hard that she was thrown ten feet away into a drainage ditch twelve feet down, and yet she was never hurt. Numerous were the times that she ran away to the woods and far fields, but never once was she shot. Once, when she was old, she lay on a hot summer's day beneath one of the farm pickups, a brown and tan Ford, and I remember still my horror as the truck bumped up and over her as she lay there in the shade. The rear tire went over her; I saw it. I carried her into the cab, and we took her to the vet, who said that X-rays showed her back was broken. The next day she came trotting home with me, wholly recovered, and sat beside me just like she always had, as if she were human.

But those were her twilight years, and it wasn't long after that she died. I remember well the incomprehension in her eyes as she lay there, unable to work properly what once had been so remarkable a body, looking for reassurance that all would be fine. She's buried out back west of the back pasture, and I don't pass that spot without recalling her. I suppose that in a world where men think little of murdering thousands of men, women, and children, the death of a dog isn't worth much pondering, and yet the truth is that my throat tightens a little even now when I think about her. It was some years before I thought about getting another dog, and a long time after that before I did so: a Border collie pup with sharp, inquisitive eyes.

Watching Sheba grow up, I couldn't help noticing what it was like to be a puppy and experience the world anew. What interesting scents there are! For a puppy, everything is noteworthy and deserves investigation. Garbage isn't garbage, but a repository of the most wonderful, rich scents—just like strange people. When I took her home, she was so small that she crawled for warmth (it was just before the winter solstice) into the sleeve of the jacket I was wearing; she would trot faithfully behind me on walks, looking for all the world like a tiny wind-up toy. I had forgotten how small a puppy is, or how quickly it grows up.

In this respect, dogs are the converse of farms, for while traditionally farms and the land long outlive any one farmer, we humans invariably outlast our dogs. Both are lessons in the transience of all things and the foolishness of believing that we can truly own anything. We are, with dogs as with land, ultimately only friends who one day meet and must perforce another day part. Dogs, in their aging and dying, remind us that this is so, but of course we mostly forget the lessons they would teach us and obdurately go on believing that we "own" the land and the dog, and some erroneously think we can do with them as we will without consequence. Perhaps our dogs are to us as we should be to the land, faithful because through it we live.

# Work and Days

We were raised on work. I suppose that we never really questioned it; I don't remember ever saying to one of my cousins—or hearing them say—that we were working too much or too hard. It was a given, as much a part of our environment as the earth itself, like an element we lived in. Hauling hay, hoeing, picking up rocks out of the fields, spreading straw on strawberries in early winter, putting brush together between the apple tree rows in winter: there's always something to do. During the time I was growing up, my extended family—uncles and cousins, mainly—came to work on the farm on Saturdays, and we all took for granted that in the summer, we'd help on the farm.

It's strange to think how almost utterly divorced from the farm was school for us. In my experience, elementary school, junior high, and high school were not work, nor play, but enforced monotony rather along the lines of penitentiary confinement (save that no one was penitent). Occasionally I had good teachers, but they were rebels, and have long since left the profession: now a carpenter, for instance, my sixth-grade teacher, a muscular, mustachioed fellow, encouraged us each to write at least a fifty-page story, no small task for a twelve-year-old, but we all accomplished it, and I remember with the accomplishment came a satisfaction that did not come again for many years. For the most part, though, we would be bussed off to school and there enter a world of cinderblock hallways and bells on the hour, of oppressive uniformity.

Little wonder that most of us became hellions—where else was there a challenge? When one is surrounded by a "system," the only recourse for the independent-minded is to violate it, and that, needless to say, is what we did. Undoubtedly the public school system in America has its functions, but education is mostly not among them. One is being prepared to be an American consumer, left adrift in a sea of students who have as few clues about where to go or what do to in life as oneself. The overpopulated classes are far from intellectually challenging, and so one longs for escape from this morass of mediocrity, seeking it aimlessly in juvenile pranks and alcohol, in drugs and violence, in sex and whatever else one can concoct to do that would crack the shell.

By contrast, the farm is a place of clear, even irrefutable values: You work, and you do it right, all of which is utterly obvious. What's more, you do it in a community whose members are joined by blood, and who have known one another all their lives. There's an unspoken acquiescence to the larger community, some of whose members are among the dead, others yet unborn, and to the place itself, too. I noticed early on—around twelve or thirteen—that my uncle who ran the farm often would ask us whether we wanted to do something, rather than issuing orders; it's subtle, but it's something you notice when you compare that to the school's shunting us from room to room in herds. One works, on the farm, of one's own free will, by common assent, for reasons that have nothing to do with consumerism or human herds. On the farm, you're an individual.

I think, though, that for us, growing up, the two worlds mingled: school, with its shiftless conformity, leaked over into the world of the farm. How could it not? You spend your days in a place whose closest architectural equivalent is a prison and it has to affect your perceptions, it has to osmose into the rest of your life, like some chemistry experiment gone wrong, its acrid scent creeping into all the surrounding rooms. Perhaps one day public education will begin finally to learn the lessons of Pestalozzi and Montessori and Steiner, but I doubt it: its purpose, after all, is to socialize, not to genuinely educate, and where genuine education takes place, the dim grow suspicious. It doesn't take much to incite the unthinking against those who question conventions. Socrates, Christ, and Bruno reveal the masses' antagonism toward the highest, which we can't ignore and which hasn't disappeared.

But there's a different kind of education you get on the farm. That education has informed all the work I've done ever since. For me and for my cousin Peter Joe, as for his brothers Steve and Dave, and my cousins Peter Phil, and Chad, it started when we were on the brink of adolescence, twelve or thirteen, and we were big enough to start lugging, meaning to carry a full half bushel basket or a peck basket of peaches from beneath a tree to the pickup truck and slide it onto the bed. About this same time, we also started lugging corn, a far harder task, and one that deserves some consideration on its own.

To lug corn you arrive at the farm before dawn, walking up the road to the white house atop the hill, cutting across the yard to the lean-to barn built into the northern hillside. That barn is gone now, burned up by an incendiary lightning strike years past, but I can imagine it still, with its dirt floor, its rough-cut crossbeams and center beams, behind it the old stagnant outhouses under the pines. We kept stacks and stacks of wooden crates in that barn, and an old Allis Chalmers combine—I've often regretted that I didn't prowl around in there more, for that was the oldest barn in the whole area, probably one of the oldest in this part of the state. "Tamarack beams," my Uncle Warren noted in his deep voice. We'd gather near that barn, or maybe near the tool shed, and stand around for a bit, talking about the weather, or sports, or the price of something. There's a photograph of us all standing together, wearing our lugging straps and heavy boots, ragged clothes, looking for all the world like we belonged to another century—the nineteenth at the latest—and I think we did.

There would be some horseplay, maybe some scurrying around to find baskets, and occasional laconic conversations, until my uncle would climb into the pickup and slam the door, spilling some coffee on the dashboard. Everyone then clambered onto the back of the truck, lining up along the bolted wooden racks, or sitting on the crossboards facing the tailgate. There's an art to getting on a moving pickup, and a kind of etiquette as well: if you're standing on the back corner, you move aside, while the fellow boarding would grasp the last metal strut of the racks and step up, almost as if he were mounting a horse, perhaps balancing with one foot on the bumper the whole way. And so we'd ride, in the wind, along the dusty two-track around to the east and then north, cutting from the trail into the cornfield, at first with only one pickup, in later years with two or more.

We'd ride between rows of sweet corn, the wide green leaves wet with dew slapping the sides of the truck, the stalks of the row beneath the truck cracking, until we reached where we ended the last time, and the truck would stop. That is when the real work started. Inasmuch as it takes experience to pick corn, we boys were luggers, and a lugger has a rough job, for he has to walk backwards between two rows of corn carrying a bushel basket held by a brown cotton strap over one shoulder, all the while using his hands to stack the corn in the bushel. Of course, the picker doesn't have it all that easy either, especially in some fields where the corn is stunted and low, for he has to bend forward, stripping the ears off the stalks with clean, quick movements, and flipping them up into the bushel.

It's not easy to do either job well, and everyone is absolutely soaking wet from dew in about five minutes. At first you notice the dew running in rivulets from the sandpaper-rough green leaves after you brush them, and soon you're aware that your hands and pants are sopping; if your pants are tucked into your boots, you soon hear a squishing sound as you walk, more even than that from the brown muck you're slogging through. Although the lugger has to carry the full weight of a laden bushel so he has to swagger backwards, still he's not as wet as the picker, and his hands don't get as chapped. A picker's hands—or at least, my hands, since not everyone has this problem—become slowly more raw and cracked, until by summer's end one has lobster claws, and is hardly able to pick up a piece of paper from a table. Your hands go through layer upon layer of white peeling skin, unfurling tattered translucent papyri, and sometimes your hands bleed or your elbow tendons hurt, but you just pick anyway, leaving traces of blood on the green-sheathed ears.

Then there's the sweet corn itself. People's standards are high nowadays—they expect their fruit and vegetables to be nigh unto perfect, as if manufactured rather than grown—so you have to pick carefully, and there is much to avoid. It's impossible to peel back every ear you pick to check it, so you have to develop a clear sense of how a ripe ear feels and looks, glimpsed out of the corner of your eye, every decision made in an instant. Some ears will be too young, still white kernels, and others will be bird-pecked or coon-chewed, or wormy, or infected by corn smut, a vile-looking gray-black fungus, and you need to recognize each of these intuitively as you pick, your hands constantly testing, tearing, tossing corn up into the bushel in a blur, or filling a crooked arm with a handful until your lugger comes back from the truck, emerging through the greenery with basket ready.

Perhaps worst are the bird pecks; they offend your sense of propriety and natural dislike of waste. For a seething flock of blackbirds, grackles, and starlings will descend like some dark biblical plague, filling surrounding trees like black leaves and sending forth emissaries to test the fields, then settling upon a field the day before harvest. From a distance you can hardly see them in the cornfield, though you hear them squawking; they clutch onto the stalks and poke their beaks through the corn's green sheath to penetrate a kernel or two, then move on to another stalk, another ear. In this way, a flock can destroy a whole field in less than an hour, certainly in a few hours, and you'll know as soon as you start to pick the corn, at first by the disheveled husks, then perhaps by the rotting kernels' smell. Sometimes you can smell a whole field rotting.

As I noted earlier, the birds' dark plague is partly our own fault: mostly not native species, these vast flocks subsist parasitically upon multi-acre crops. But our fields are not huge—they can't be, since we pick by hand, not machines—and are tailored to the landscape, a few acres here, a few there, from the air a tiny patchwork of orchard and field, passed over in but a few moments. So although the birds will descend on one field or another, perhaps our corn-fields are offering to rectify the distorted patterns of life that our civilization has created. In any case the birds do not descend on all the fields; they move on to another farm, to another landscape miles and miles away, perhaps frightened by our shotguns, or by our booming little carbide cannon used to scare them off.

But back to work. When I was a boy, we usually picked per-haps fifty or a hundred bushels of sweet corn a day, unloading the last truckload onto the cement floor of our red pole barn fruit market along the highway, and then going off to the coffee shop. By that time—perhaps eight-thirty in the morning—we were pretty rough looking, all wet and raw, with dirt-encrusted sopping pants and, if it was a warm morning, tangled sweaty hair. It must have made a strange sight, all of us sitting on the back of the truck, leaning against the racks, talking loudly into the wind as we rolled by suburban houses to the coffee shop, then back from the coffee shop to the fruit stand or out to the peach orchard.

Sometimes at the fruit stand we would unload the truckload of fresh peaches or sweet corn and then briefly catch our breath, a group of sunburned boys and men in tattered clothes, wearing picking straps and looking as if we belonged to a different century. Sometimes, in the fruitstand or in the field, one of my uncles would tell some anecdote that had us all laughing. I have a photograph of such a moment: my father, my uncles, Jim Van Dyken, and stocky Abe Moerland (a son of our great-grandfather's eldest daughter Jess, and a farmer himself) laughing uproariously in the midst of a day's labors. Farm work affords many such moments, punctuation to the cadenced sentences of work.

One summer we had a Peace Corps volunteer come to work with us. He was a tall, stringy, dark-haired fellow with a sallow complexion, and an eagerness to learn about farming. Although he had grown up in the suburbs, he had gone and volunteered to live in some obscure little African country, where evidently the Peace Corps was going to instruct the locals on how they could adapt their subsistence farming traditions to American methods, undoubtedly to everyone's detriment. I remember him standing uneasily off to the side one morning when we assembled at the main farm house before picking corn. His car, a battered old green Ford Fairlane, was parked alongside the big barn, and he had to move it under an apple tree to get it out of the way. He was wearing jeans, a T-shirt, and jogging shoes.

We drove out to the cornfield below the main house, and all jumped off the truck, fanning out, everybody taking his usual place, luggers backing up, readying bushels, pickers testing the first ears, stripping them back to see what the corn looked like. My Uncle Dave had the fellow lug for him, and I remember clearly how he looked around at the rest of us—he wanted to do it right. He adjusted his strap to lower the basket, and did his best to place the ears. It's hard to pick with a green lugger, mainly because you have to do much of the work of stacking the bushel yourself. Lugging might look like any lunk could do it, but the truth is, it takes a fair amount of skill—and strength.

The strength necessary is why I mention this episode. Two-thirds of the way through our second truckload, the Peace Corps volunteer looked as if he were going to die. He leaned forward like a winded runner, hands on his knees, strap and empty basket hanging down. "Do you guys always work like this?" he asked one of my cousins, who was lumbering by with a full bushel. "Pretty much," somebody said. It was muddy that day, and you had to force your way through the muck and between the tall stalks, all the while getting wetter and scruffier. True, my cousins are big and athletic, but this fellow wasn't in poor condition; he just wasn't used to doing this kind of work. By the time we got to the coffee shop he looked like he had barely survived the Vietnam War that morning—he appeared haggard—and when we gulped down coffee and drove out to the peaches, he looked even more stricken. Word was that he left, hiked across the fields to his car, and went home to recuperate. Sure enough, when we went up at noon his car was gone, and we never saw him again. I mention this episode because it was the first time I realized how the work that we took for granted might appear to an outsider.

What's the value of this work? In the *Bhagavad Gita*, Krishna tells Arjuna that work rightly done is essential to the cosmos, that there is indeed a kind of liberation through work. Krishna also points out that working outside one's destined station in life is inherently destructive, but nowadays it's hard to tell what one's appointed work is. What difficulty the young student has, trying to distinguish which occupation he ought to pursue! Of course, the word *occupation* is itself revealing, for it indicates that one is merely "occupied," that one's work is by no means destined and important to universal order, but only an exchangeable commodity like pork bellies.

In good work there is a satisfaction, and sometimes also a triumph over oneself. Occasionally, such a triumph is almost inexplicable, like the time my uncle said I should disk under a field of weeds over by the state farm across the highway. I remember well driving the tractor—a squatty, bright green John Deere with a throaty engine—and the clattering disk behind me, over the four-lane highway and down the two-track dirt road to the field. When I arrived, I pushed in the clutch with my left foot and stopped for a moment: that field was golden with ragweed, to which I have been allergic for years. Behind me was the disk, green-painted bars with silver metal circles poised by a hydraulic system, ready to sink into the earth. If I drove forward, I'd be driving into allergy hell.

I let out the clutch, lowered the disk as the tractor surged forward, and behind me rose clouds of yellow pollen, like some bizarre fog rising golden against a clear blue summer sky. The wind carried that golden mist toward me, then away from me as I circled. When you disk a field it seems at first that the work will take forever, that you'll be making round after round into infinity—but then, slowly, you make your way across in strips, arcs that eventually bring you inevitably to the field's edge. When I finished, the tractor, my legs, my face, my hair, all were a bright yellow: pollen lay in ridges along the disk's frame, and tinged even the thick black shoulder-high rubber tires. But only my eyes burned a bit.

To this day, I cannot explain why I didn't go into anaphylactic shock from such an overdose of pollen. Perhaps it was the sheer volume of it, so much that my system couldn't even recognize it as an allergen anymore; or perhaps as I've grown older, I've gained immunities. It might also be that my determination, my sheer will to finish the task, had somehow rendered me immune. Hard to say. But there was satisfaction in seeing those weeds flattening behind me. When the field was completely civilized, I left, with red eyes and a bout of sneezing, driving back to the main house where I parked the tractor and dismounted. My cousin Ned was there, tall and chuckling, and he said: "What happened to you?" "Disked down that ragweed." As I walked away, I glanced back at the yellow tractor.

I suppose this episode, one of countless work stories I could tell, is so memorable because it represents a kind of triumph over myself and over adverse circumstances. Perhaps all work finally comes down to such an overcoming, but this is not work at its best, by any means. I remain ambivalent about this episode. At its best, work isn't a conquest, but a natural conjoining with one's surroundings through doing; it is a kind of spiritual union through action. I don't mean to belittle the satisfaction born of triumph, but surely the best work is something like play, into which one is completely absorbed, and which when it's finished leaves little trace, though somehow the world behind one has been made better.

Surely this is what Lao Tsu meant by *wu wei*, "work without doing," the highest form of work. I have experienced this too. For instance, sometimes on a tractor you will hardly take notice of time, particularly if driving requires constant attentiveness, continual glancing back at your left rear side, one hand perched on the fender or the hydraulic control, the other on the wheel. Work without doing is not only to be found in bucolic scenes; it is a state of consciousness, and I can imagine a pilot or a computer user who is as deeply into work as the character Levin in *Anna Karenina*, out working with his scythe among the peasants, oblivious to worries of the world.

The difference is, of course, that the pilot or the computer user isn't touching the earth, and it is not very many steps to the delusion that the earth isn't valuable any more. There's something especially salutary about hoeing and pulling out weeds—no one doing this work is likely to get sucked into a virtual reality faery realm and not come out again. Because while it's possible to enter into a state of *wu wei* as you hoe, your consciousness is always grounded in the earth in which you're working, under the sky and sun and in the breeze. You are working the earth, between earth and sky, the place of mankind since first we emerged from the Garden into the garden.

As modern humanity slowly forgets where fruits and vegetables come from, work like hoeing becomes all the more important. For one who hoes is forging a link not only between earth and sky, but with human antiquity, with those who hoed six thousand years ago. Modern people are largely conditioned against ordinary labor like this—everyone wants to be kings and queens (albeit without responsibility) and no one wants to be a peasant. Peasantry has gotten a bad reputation in modernity—we're all too ready to see the past as a dark age and only our own era as enlightened. I wouldn't be surprised if the last man—standing on a heap of burnt garbage, debris smoldering as far as the eye can see—still insisted that history had reached its highest point in him. Might it not be better to hoe, to help the earth be fruitful?

There are, nowadays, reactionaries who look at the wreckage left behind by our "progress" and reject the whole of civilization, insisting that even agriculture is decadent. To these purists, only complete inaction, only utterly leaving everything alone, is enough. Perhaps this is so, in the end, and the wisest of us are those who do not seek to change the world but to leave it alone. After all, there is always the lure of the mountains and becoming a recluse, living in a cave or some secluded hermitage. Still, if we wish to maintain a community, we must needs have our labors, our obligation to hoe the earth, to trim the trees, to do the work that our ancestors did and our grandchildren must also do. There is an inextinguishable nobility and goodness in authentic work.

But all work is not the same. For instance, whereas my great-grandfather had little to do with chemicals, contemporary farmers and farmworkers feel they must plunge into what seems a veritable ocean of pesticides, fungicides, and herbicides, some of which are truly deadly, or else scab infections or codling moths will attack the apples, and then finicky buyers will purchase apples from somewhere else, most likely somewhere without any pesticide regulation at all, and with workers paid a dime an hour.

I grew up hearing the howl of spray rigs in the distance, and it is a familiar and reassuring sound. Dave's on his sprayer and all's right with the world. You think that I'm joking, but I'm serious—there's even an art to locating someone spraying off in the distance. You shut off your pickup and listen intently, scarcely breathing, then drive in their direction, looking for that mist blown up like whale blasts above the trees. When you finally see it—and often it takes a while—you calculate how long it'll be before he gets to row's end, and where you ought to park so that he will see you when he turns and will have time to shut her down. If he decides to get off, first he'll cut the power to that hundred-mile-an-hour airblast engine on the big red tube sprayer, streaked with white, and then as it putters to a stop, he'll clamber down. A tiny spurt of milky fluid will drip from the bottom jets, and when he gets into the truck, an exotic odor will waft inside with him and remain, something alien and unnatural.

Perhaps, if it's an insecticide he's spraying, he'll casually unclasp his black mask with its two large round filters where his mouth would be, let it fall down to his neck, perhaps even take off the heavy jacket he's wearing for protection. But still that scent will linger. And you'll talk of the baseball standings or of the latest foolishness in Washington, or of a fox that someone saw at the end of a row. Maybe mention how much is left in the tank, or how much orchard there is left to spray, or what the wind's doing. You'll only rarely talk about the actual work, no more than guys in the military would talk about their work—it's just something that you do, disagreeable or not. I'm not even sure what good it would do to talk about it, because with hundreds of acres to spray, you do what you have to do.

But I, sitting here now in my study, have the luxury of thinking about these things, about the terrible dilemmas with which our society daily confronts us. Nowhere are these dilemmas writ clearer than in this question of chemicals. For pesticides are required in order to grow modern varieties of apples, the kinds that you purchase in the stores, and so the grower is caught very much as a drug user is caught: he has to have his supply. And of course the chemical companies foster this dependence, supporting the agricultural research in the universities that brings forth new varieties of fruit trees that also require spraying. What's more, once such fruit trees are in the ground and the old ones are cut down, it's not like a grower can just up and switch: he's stuck, at least for a while.

There's plenty of hysteria about these chemicals, and this only adds to the farmer's dilemma. For suddenly he's depicted as some kind of technobarbarian, irrevocably poisoning the natural world. Often the very people who haven't a clue where an apple comes from, and who purchase fruit from some foreign country where DDT is still used, suddenly shriek completely unfounded complaints about a local farmer. One young fellow chased my cousin Peter Joe down and chewed him out for letting a tiny bit of spray blow from the bottom nozzle of the spray rig onto the fender of his car as he blasted by the tractor and rig at sixty miles an hour. What did this young fellow think? That the spray would insidiously make its way from the fender inside the car and climb up inside his pants leg like a tick?

An eighty-year-old orchardist I know was out spraying for scab infection on a breezy spring day, and a neighbor called the state to complain that he was spraying chemicals in the wind. Now, not only was he not spraying anything dangerous, he was driving an old orange Allis Chalmers tractor while his son used a small spray gun on young trees—the rough equivalent of a glorified garden hose. "But they don't know," he said. "They've never set foot on a farm; they don't know what I was spraying; they don't know what a spray gun is; and they don't know that you can't always sit around and wait for the wind to die down. But they're the same people who want perfect apples in the store. So I signed the little piece of paper that said I was spraying in the wind, and the woman from the agriculture department or whatever it was went away." He folded his hands over his worn overalls and shook his head. "People." And he smiled the smile of an eighty-year-old man who had seen it all.

But how do we account for the fact that he has spent much of his life working with poisonous chemicals, often barehanded, and has rarely even been sick? Perhaps his immunity comes from being in nature all the time, out of doors and under the sun. It is a fact that chemicals break down in direct sunlight, yet even beyond this, I believe that people who are outside daily in the green, out in the wind and sun, have a natural vitality. They draw life from life; or perhaps, life offers them gifts that those who live only indoors refuse. It may well be that those who live outdoors all day and work with the earth become earthy—and the earth always accepts, the earth bears; its munificence seems boundless.

Still, that my elderly friend made it to eighty doesn't mean we all will, nor will nature forever absorb our filth without consequences. We humans tend to ignore our future, and, seeking to save our present way of life, we relinquish our future. It is almost a cliché that modernity is a parasite upon its children's children. The earth's back is broad, and it can bear much, yet already we can see changes in the weather patterns, rains coming erratically, first droughts, then floods, burning heat and bitter cold, earthquakes as the land seeks to shake off the burdensome buildings and paved carapace, the poisons and garbage. While we may not immediately see all the results of what we now do, we surely one day will reap what we sow. Of that I have no doubt whatever.

And surely one would think the farmer would lead the way toward conserving for his children's children's children. He knows better than anyone the danger of these pesticides. But he is in a bind, for it is hard to see how to farm hundreds of acres without them. And so the very people whose motivation is naturally to preserve the land and its fertility are by dint of circumstance driven inevitably to sign that same devil's bargain year after year with one agrochemical company or another, always with that sinking feeling that Faust must have felt, that intuition of something wrong from the very beginning. Still, for him, the earth is accepting, willing to bear up for this one more year.

Yet we know—we all know, every one of us—that this cannot go on. By this I mean that the whole modern consumerist juggernaut—the relentless destruction of all the things we can love or cherish, the obliteration of all the most meaningful things, the vistas, the woods and waters, the orchards and lakes, the owls and hawks and frogs and foxes, this destruction of life in the name of greed and power—cannot go on forever. It must stop. The special dilemma of the farmer is that he who has the most at stake, who most of all must preserve the land, feels compelled to use deadly poisons on it, on the green and growing things, and therefore even on himself. But this dilemma cannot last: we will move toward balance.

For the orchardist, the path beyond chemicals is arduous. It is not as though we could suddenly stop using chemicals and still grow the same kind of fruit. Delicious, McIntosh, Empire, Rome: these are the most popular varieties of apples, but they are also the most disease-prone, and poorest for storage. So the apple grower will have to plant different kinds of apples, "antique" or recently created varieties whose resistance to disease is far higher than that of modern varieties. But this is no small investment—with no guarantee that people will want to purchase long-storing, disease-resistant apples like Nigers or Hubbardstons, names familiar only to their great-grandparents.

Of course, part of the problem lies with modern people's requirements. Our grandparents didn't mind an occasional blemish in fruit. But people insist nowadays that their fruit be perfect, that their apples be large, lustrous, richly colored, with nary a worm or a scab or a sting in sight. I have seen women shriek and drop an ear of sweet corn as if the devil himself had peeked from behind the ear's brown-haired tip, when in fact it was only a harmless gray earworm peering up to see what the fuss was all about. "Good God! What is *this* doing here?" someone shouts, not realizing how many pesticide sprays one must apply to a field in order to have totally worm-free corn. Perfection comes with a very high price for us all: in the end, the price will be too high.

# That Old-Time Religion

White-painted clapboard, a square, stolid building with a small steeple on one corner of the roof, two narrow high windows, and simple doors flung open, outside which you can see the horses and wagons patiently waiting, waiting now, in this photograph, for more than a century. If you were to go inside, you'd see bare burnished wooden pews upon which sit sunburned men in stiff suits and shirts, women wearing long dresses and bonnets, while in front there'd be a minister preaching, a stern-looking man wearing a black robe, perhaps speaking in Dutch, probably haranguing the congregation or attacking the decline in society, while children fidget and gaze curiously at their transfixed elders, attempting to stay still more to avoid their neighbors' censure than out of fascination with the sermon.

So it was in those days when families and communities lived their lives around a single church, when the Calvinist religion of the Old World was practiced more intensely here than in Holland itself. It's a curious fact that expatriate communities are, as a rule, more conservative than those of their originating country, that language and customs extinct in the Netherlands may be alive in America. Certainly it's true that the Netherlands as a whole is far more liberal than the American-Dutch communities I'm familiar with—as if the cultural erosion inherent in American life should somehow inspire as compensation a fierce desire among some Americans to maintain dikes and bulwarks against such erosion. I think of the immigrant woman who died not long ago at eighty-two, most of those years lived on the west side of Grand Rapids—and who never spoke English at all.

How difficult it is to maintain such barriers in America, because the new is always seductive—not for the elderly, of course, but for the young, for the next generation, and the next. I grew up in a loosely Calvinist world, uncles and aunts and cousins and grand-parents who shared a common understanding of who we were and how we ought to live. Undoubtedly, our world was far from that of the clapboard church outside which horses patiently waited, but it was equally far from that of what I call the suburban-American vac-uum, the Nothing. We stood, in those days, midway between the Old World and the New. Some still do.

Not long ago I visited a Calvinist church that had separated from its mother church because of what its founding members perceived as backsliding in the mainstream denomination. It was a bracing experience, attending their services, which were full of the vim that only comes from reactionary convictions. Sitting in the pew alongside me were neatly dressed rows of children and par-ents, the children sitting primly and silently, all of us listening to a piercingly harsh sermon on the decline of American morals. It's interesting that the full force of the preacher's gale lashed not just the rubbish on television (a predictable target), but even more the failure of the mainstream denomination itself.

There is something attractive in a prophetic voice, insisting that the chosen people have forsaken the true way and gone off into worshipping idols again—it is an old story, to be sure, but you can dust it off and apply it to an age of technology well enough if you like. In fact, in an age of relativism, an era when nihilism is just another choice like any other, when ways of thought can be lined up on supermarket shelves and whichever one you choose is fine by us, it's refreshing to find people who insist that there is right and wrong, that even if everyone else in the whole world were to go traipsing off after the will-o'-the-wisp of evolutionary theory, we wouldn't. I have sympathy with people who refuse to go along with the herd.

What was it Crèvecoeur said two centuries ago in his *Letters from an American Farmer*? America is filled with little sects, sects of one, sometimes—every man who grows dissatisfied with some doctrinal point in his church goes off to found another. There is still some truth in this observation today. And yet I think a child raised in a congregation grows up without thinking there are other ways, or that one might dissent on this or that point and found a new sect or denomination. One accepts what is there, even if it sometimes seems unreasonable, simply because as a child it is all one knows. When does this change? Probably when one becomes a cantankerous old man or woman, that's when.

I have known some pretty cantankerous old Calvinists, and know others by repute, for they sometimes throw a large shadow. Sometimes they're not so old, either—like a young man I'll call David, a fellow in his thirties, with tousled brown hair and a lanky build who's a Nederdite. Nederdites are fairly strict, as a rule, shunning dancing and films and other worldly distractions. But David goes beyond this. Because he and his family don't believe in the power of the state, he won't take oaths, and in particular, he won't get a driver's license or insurance. His family doesn't believe in insurance; if they have problems that cost more money than they have, then the family will take care of it.

One day not too long ago, David's practice of driving without a license attracted the attention of a policeman, who took him down to the county jail. So David sat in jail. "If you'll just go get a license and insurance," said the police, "we'll let you out." "How long can you afford to keep me here?" David replied, expressionless. It was a draw: one bullheaded Calvinist against the police department and the judge. It lasted nearly a week, and then they let him out; his brothers picked him up, drove his truck home for him, and the following day, he resumed his daily business.

Now what are you to make of a character like this? It's true that I don't necessarily want people without driver's licenses or insurance driving on the road beside me. But I can't deny a certain affection for someone like this: while I wouldn't want a whole society of such characters, I'm happy to know that there's *someone* out there whose personal code of ethics utterly transcends those of the rest of us. He's not licenseless because he's trying to get away with some crime or another—I've no doubt at all that he'd sooner give up everything he has than commit a crime. Such a fellow is an implacable moral force, willing to go to jail rather than compromise his principles, however eccentric they might seem to us.

Of course, the same implacability has a certain ridiculous quality to it, reminding us of Don Quixote riding full tilt against a windmill, Don Quixote remembered as high comedy, but in fact also bearing a kind of chivalric grandeur and dignity recognizable even in our desiccated machine-society. I am also reminded of an elderly local businessman who conceived an ever greater disgust for the fact that Calvin College has had to teach some semblance of evolutionary theory. Hence, in the late twentieth century, people in Grand Rapids were treated to the spectacle of full-page newspaper advertisements decrying Calvin College's falling away from the true faith, and calling it back from teaching evolution.

Now, it's true that one can see such advertisements as anachronistic, but although I confess to an initial dislike for them, I have eventually come to see them as rather entertaining and even admirable. Many people undoubtedly have somewhat prematurely concluded that the evolutionism-creationism debate was settled in 1925 with the Scopes trial, but of course that was only a single victory in a much longer and more widespread war whose ultimate victor has by no means yet raised the final flag over the enemy's last bastion. I'm not endorsing creationism here—there are much more subtle alternatives—but certainly there are some grounds for the instinctive recognition by many people that evolution as a theory is intrinsically opposed to religion.

If we're schooled in modern ways, why, attacking evolutionary theory may seem like a quixotic effort, quaint, like claiming that the world is flat, or that the sun actually rises each day. But although I've been schooled in these modern ways too, I've come to see that they too are transitory, that while today evolutionary theory may seem like the end-all of insights, it is in fact just a theory, a construct that people have created and embraced by consensus, acceding to it just as they once acceded to the view that the sun actually rises—which of course, from a terrene perspective, it actually does. Theories and hypotheses change like fashions in clothing, and however much they may seem like an incontrovertible norm, in fact they are but the infatuations of a generation, of no more ultimate consequence than the kind of trousers men wear.

And yet it is rare for someone to reach the point of recognizing this, even rarer to advertise it to the world, inviting ridicule like some knight of La Mancha who refuses to give up his chivalric code even in a world of scornful shopkeepers and factory peasants. What an inner certainty it takes to insist like Thoreau that we must each decide for ourselves where we stand, and be willing to flout the masses' opinions even if it cost us our lives. There is in such an insistence something intrinsically American, owing much to the Puritans whose spirit still permeates occasional pockets of American society despite centuries of rampant mercantilism and now consumerism.

Needless to say, there's a continuum on which one can place Puritanism as a predecessor to modern consumerism, seeing mercantilism as a parody of the Calvinist view that one's outward station in life can reflect God's favor. We gather worldly goods, our wealth supposedly revealing our righteousness Yet in consumerism there is no salvation, there is only accumulation, only outward show, from which even the idea of divine favor has disappeared. Consumerism, one might say, is the shell left behind when religion departed, and its consolations are unquestionably this-worldly.

But Puritans, those early-American Calvinists, were not such prudes and hypocrites as some might think, and even if they were, theirs was nonetheless a religion among whose adherents walked lovers of God, even God-intoxicated mystics. It's true that the history books often show us only grim men and women dressed in black, who occasionally killed people, yet there's a wholly different side to the Puritans that's accessible only infrequently, through original documents, in which spiritual life was a living reality, permeating daily life, filling them with joy. I think of Sarah Pierrepont—later wife of the eighteenth-century minister Jonathan Edwards—who as a young girl, after a conversion experience, wandered the fields and woods filled with love for all creatures and people. She was not alone, for though it is easy to ignore this side of Calvinism, it existed.

It is telling that Edwards wrote such a loving description of an inspired woman who in some ways presages American Transcendentalism, for of course he is most well known for his fevered sermons, most notably the terrifying "Sinners in the Hands of an Angry God." How can we reconcile this fire-and-brimstone oration with the gentle beauty of other Edwards prose? Strange as it may seem, I believe that these two sides are necessary for one another—that the fear of wrath and damnation complements and can even bring about its polar opposite, a loving peacefulness. We forget that Edwards's fierce Calvinist sermons frightened some—but this fear often brought about a deep and lasting inward transformation, a shift from trepidation to illumination.

Indeed, I'll go even further here, and suggest that there are profound parallels between Calvinist "conversion literature" and accounts of spiritual crisis and subsequent illumination in Zen Buddhism and other traditions. Certainly it is noteworthy that the hell-and-damnation sermons had the effect of throwing people into crisis, into doubting their own conventional religious beliefs, and forcing them toward direct spiritual experience, toward throwing themselves upon divine mercy. And the experiences of subsequent grace and illumination, like these crises preceding them, have their direct parallels in very recent Buddhist accounts of spiritual doubt, crisis, and awakening. While we might like to dismiss Calvinists as conventional and social, motivated by what others think about them, in fact there is a much deeper tradition of inward focus and redemption whose importance is evidently inconvenient for inclusion in history books.

Much of Calvinism that seems quaint or archaic may in fact be like the residue or hardened rind of what was once living experience. For instance, while the doctrine of predestination is often interpreted as buttressing the social order and as a nearly monstrous principle according to which God decides in advance who goes to heaven and who to hell, in fact we could read this same doctrine in very different ways: first, as the formulation of how the Divine—wholly beyond past, present, and future—must by definition know all things, including the ultimate destinies of all beings, and second, as a way of encouraging people to see themselves always in danger, never absolutely knowing that they will attain salvation, hence remaining humble.

We too easily ignore the experiential side of Calvinism, which for all its stringent logic and doctrinal complexities nonetheless had a mystical streak running through it. One wonders how often these doctrines might have emerged from mighty efforts to wrestle the human mind around illuminations, or how often these doctrines might have served only to obscure the center of the tradition, which (one would think) was in spiritual awakening. It might well be that hidden in Calvinism is some vast and fiery illumination, blasting the mind like a white-hot furnace suddenly revealed, uncompromising and incomprehensible. If this is so, then these doctrines that we take for the tradition are more like metal between us and it.

I have always thought that Emerson and Thoreau—indeed, virtually all of the great nineteenth-century American writers—owed a great debt to Calvinism as something they could rebel against, at the same time that they took much from it. For after all, wasn't Calvinism's context, its ambience, like soil out of which these "ultimate Protestants" could grow? Even today, America bears within it threads of Calvinism, woven through the national character, although our individualism is itself something like the national religion. It is foolish to ignore how very much we exist in a continuum, our present lives subtly shaped and informed by those of others who have been dead a hundred or a thousand years. Like plants, we thrive in the soil composed of the dead.

I count myself fortunate to have been born into a Dutch-Calvinist ambience, as if into another century, and hope that this particular culture may continue, for, whatever its flaws, it is far, far better than the consumerist standardization and nothingness that most people today are left with, the cultureless suburban vacuum, the Nothing. And yet even while writing these words, I know that the coming world has little room for such diversions from the Nothing, that even if it did, the admixture of so many traditions in modern America means that ours cannot survive entirely intact, nor can I ever really be wholly Calvinist myself. It is more like a way of seeing the world that one inherits, aspects of character and outlook and language, and perhaps these things will continue for generations to come.

Not long ago, I was asked to describe Dutch Calvinists, and after I thought about it for a bit, I replied that while it's easy to sneer at or attack Calvinism, especially if one is familiar mainly with caricatures or stereotypes, Calvinists are different than these would suggest. Calvinists on the whole tend to be hardheaded and respect erudition, preferably filtered through a Calvinist lens. Above all, Calvinists are deeply aware of human frailty, and this creates a warm, tolerant side as well as a judgmental one sometimes; they tend to be very deeply grounded in family; they tend to be disciplined, assiduous workers; and they are stubborn.

I mean stubborn—bullheaded. Frankly, I think that if you want to understand Calvinist psychology, you'd go a long way by recognizing that bullheadedness is a greater motivating force than anything else. If you make a Hollander angry, you'll see what I'm talking about. An angry Dutchman is not a reasonable Dutchman—and the only way to assuage his anger is to let him simmer until finally he blows up. You'll know that the episode is over when he's able to laugh about whatever ridiculous thing he did—of course, that might be twenty years later. Rarely has the adage about cutting off one's nose to spite one's face been more richly illustrated than among us.

Let me offer a few examples. Some years ago, the price of strawberries dropped—local and regional growers got engaged in a price war, and the newspaper-advertised price of berries that visitors picked in the field themselves just kept dropping. Along with this, local grocers refused to pay a decent wholesale price for berries, and so our berries were in danger of rotting. Rotting berries have a peculiar, almost palpable scent that hangs over a field, a purple haze, sweet and cloying under a hot June sun on a humid Michigan afternoon, as if the unpicked berries had released their scented souls into the atmosphere. It's not a scent any grower wants to detect wafting in on a breeze.

What to do? What to do, as you watch local growers undercut one another, as berries come flooding in from somewhere far away, from California or Mexico, and your local berries aren't sold to the local market? There's nothing you can do, of course, and so my uncle did the next best thing: he put an advertisement in the paper selling our berries—mind you, berries that required spreading straw in the fall and removing the straw from the plants in the spring, that required hoeing and cultivating and irrigation, fertilizing and much more, all costly—for a nickel a quart, pick your own. If people want to sell berries cheap, well then, let them match this!

I well remember the rows of cars and pickup trucks, the over-weight ladies and balding men, the mothers herding three or four duckling children, the bent, thin elderly women, the surly adolescents directed by their parents, all picking their quart baskets full to heaping, carrying them out of the field to their cars' trunks and back seats. Occasionally people would say, with concern in their eyes, "I can't pay you that little—here's fifty cents a quart, just like always." But mostly people would pay their nickels and take their berries with nary a second thought for the rich green wide strawberry rows across which they strode. At the time, I remember thinking it a pity, for those were fine, big, maroon berries, but as a fellow told my father at the time, "What better way to get publicity and gain customers?"

On the whole, I'd say that this stubbornness is responsible for the chief Calvinist virtue, if virtue it is: work for work's sake. It's not that we love to work, exactly—it's more that our iron will has us working no matter what. Several of my relatives had so much sick time accumulated by their retirement that they could have been absent from work with pay for a year or two. A school administrator, my father missed two days of work in over three decades; in college, I never missed a single day of classes. In this clan, there's a kind of religious value placed on work, on meeting or exceeding commitments.

For farmwork requires indefatigable labor, and if it doesn't, we labor anyway, just because. Perhaps you've seen the piles of stones along the edges of woods, here and there around a farm. Where do you think those stones came from, and how did they get there? A century ago, a man, perhaps a man and his boys, walked over a dusty field, picking up stones and tossing them onto a wagon being pulled by a team of calm-eyed workhorses. It takes a long time to pick up all the stones in a field, and as soon as you plow it again, you'll turn up new ones, so that even a century of plowings later if you walked that same field, you'd still find stones that you could toss onto a trailer pulled by a tractor. Your hands will be gray and smooth, your fingernails black crescents, and your hamstrings will hurt—just like those of folks a century before.

Farmwork, in short, is based in pure labor. You don't very often try to decide the relative value of what you're doing, you just do it—you just go out and trim the trees, or clear the field of stones, or push the brush into a pile, or hoe the row of strawberries, or grub (clear a space around) the young trees, and you don't think twice about it. It's a relentless kind of discipline that doesn't necessarily transfer well into modern society. By this I mean that if you hoe a row of beans, there are no other issues involved—you just hoe them, and that's that. You usually aren't faced with a moral dilemma by just going to work.

In modern society, much of our work doesn't have this pure quality—for instance, in some jobs, such as military contracts, you'd be doing the world a favor if you stalled a little. A day missed there is a couple less dead children, a few less grieving mothers. And there are many other jobs that are equally problematic— indeed, the word "job" itself is emblematic of the problem here. I taught at a university that reminded me, from time to time, of a factory, and I used to make jokes about working on the student drill press. While pure work is good—in this case, the living encounter between students and professor—work becomes impure to the degree that we are separated from what we do, from its meaning and consequences. If it's just a job, it's not good work any more, and you shouldn't do it.

If we are doing the work to which we were born, that is one thing, but it is another entirely to work assiduously in the service of a Stalin or a Mao. Ah, you might say, but these two are dead, and we live in the land of the free. Perhaps so, perhaps not, I would respond, but the danger remains that our virtues might be put to the service of vice. We must consider well who our master is, and for whom we toil. I am not at all convinced that a man who unthinkingly goes to work every day punctually—and his daily work is to sell land mines that blow the feet off children, or to convince farmers to sell their acreage for some sleazy construction project—is going to end up in paradise as a result of his assiduity.

It is all too easy to believe that simply attending church somehow confers sanctity, so that during the week one can do any damned thing one pleases. A Dutch farmer I know rather well said to me once, "Most of these people would rather steal a million dollars and give a hundred thousand to the church than earn nine hundred thousand without exploiting other people or the earth. Some of them would sell their mother and tithe part of the proceeds to the church so as to feel holy afterward." I suppose that this is the side of Calvinism that onlookers react so strongly against, that mantle of piety draped over worldly accumulation.

Even so, I'd still contend that it's far better to have a community centered on a church than to have the Nothing that threatens to overwhelm us all nowadays. For however much hypocrisy and cant you may find in a church, you'll still find some kindness there, it can still bestow some meaning to life; there's still an affirmation of transcendence at least possible within it. Outside it, out in the Land of the Nothing, there's no such affirmation or meaning, only cacophonous music and nihilist literature, people scrabbling for more money and power. Perhaps the greatest danger is that the Nothing is inside the church itself nowadays, and so even where it looks as if there might be a refuge from our demented society, there is in reality only more of the same.

What is religion, really? It is not belief, and though we may call it faith and knowing, religion is beyond these; it is the simplest and most natural thing in the world, like the wind that blows over the grass and the waters, rippling them. Religion is like the soil, like the sun and the rain, for in it we grow and become who we really are. Rilke once wrote in a letter that religion "is not duty and not renunciation, not restriction: in the infinite extent of the universe it is a direction of the heart." He continues, in a beautiful and profound passage: "However a man may proceed, wandering right or left, stumbling, falling, and getting up, doing wrong here and suffering wrong there. . . all this passes into the great religions and upholds and enriches in them the God that is their center." What is more, even one who lives on the "outermost periphery of such a circle belongs to this mighty center."

Have we come so far from that little white-painted clapboard church where we started? I wonder. Certainly we live in a different world, and I do not think we can go back, not any of us, not really. Even those who react against modernity and affirm an ever more "orthodox" reactionary faith do so in a modern context that renders their effort one among countless faiths and absences of faith. Perhaps what we need now, more than anything, is a spirituality vast enough to encompass all the myriad contradictions of our lives, to guide us not away from the earth but toward a wiser and more loving relation with it. In the end, I think that the lessons of farming, the discipline and the faith that it requires, are in themselves religious, and so long as we recognize these, we will not be far off nor far mistaken, whatever happens in "the world."

# Tree of Knowledge, Tree of Life

It's a discussion that occasionally comes up when we're out hoe-ing on a hot July day under an endless azure sky, and we've worn out contemporary politics, and sports, and other ephemeral con-cerns. Hoeing can put an edge on existential matters: How is it that we've got weeds and sin to contend with? My Uncle Warren might ask the question, pausing between plants, maybe resting a thick hand on the top of his hoe handle and looking over at, say, Jim Van Dyken with a sly expression, almost bemused. A question like that doesn't exactly require an *answer* so much as a reply; in the asking as in the replying, there's a kind of mutual affirmation of community, of shared experience and knowledge.

What's the reply? Whatever it might be, it's grounded in Genesis, and in the fall from Eden. The agrarian nature of the Old Testament in its first book isn't sufficiently appreciated anymore: but nearly every central image is to be found in daily agricultural life. Chief among these images are, of course, the two trees: the tree of knowledge of good and evil, and the tree of life. It's said of some early Gnostic sects that they reverse the conventional sym-bolism of these trees, making of Adam and Eve's tasting the fruit of knowledge not a fall, but an awakening; according to them, the real fall consisted in the demiurge driving the awakened Adam and Eve out of the earthly paradise. Such an interpretation might not sit well with Calvinists, who are marked perhaps above all by an awareness of original sin, but it has the advantage, at least, of *being* an interpretation.

Many, perhaps most, today don't have the luxury of multiple interpretations, of seeing this profound symbolism in new ways. In my experience teaching in college, most people don't know Genesis well enough to discuss it. It's true you'll find an occasional Bible reader, but nowhere near enough of them to assume that an allusion to it would be widely recognized. In fact, I've had entire literature classes, purportedly including Christians, who did not know Jeremiah, nor the term *jeremiad*, nor the name Noah, nor the parable of the prodigal son. I've two conclusions that I draw out of this: first, that without these common references, we have no common culture; and second, that we already live in a post-Christian, and for many people a post-religious, world.

So bear with me. I grew up on an anachronistic isle of Dutch Calvinist farmers perhaps closer to the world of the Calvinist settlers in New England several centuries before than to the cynical, fragmented era that people claim is defined by information. The information age, they call ours, yet it seems to me that we are increasingly distant from information—which, after all, in-forms—but are awash in oceans of virtually meaningless data. Now, when you think about the two trees in the garden of Eden as you hoe, you're thinking about two symbols, two images that link the world around you—with its own tangible trees—to its spiritual origin. The trees in Eden inform the trees we see, how we see them, and how we see each other.

What happens when all these bonds are sundered? Think about what I'm asking here; think about this little vignette. Hand labor is mostly sneered at in modern society, but here we are, hoeing a field of newly planted strawberries, in the faith that they will bear fruit in a year or two. Hoeing is as archaic an activity as most people are likely to do; Adam and Eve and family undoubtedly hoed shortly after being booted out of Eden, as someone is likely to point out in our conversation, and people have been doing so ever since, all the passing generations down to the present. In this world, everything is connected: family, the land, the plants, spirituality. You can't take out one; they are indisseverably linked.

But although we live in a world where lip service is sometimes paid to these linked elements in a complete life, the truth is that mostly people today delegate them and the possibility of their continuance to someone else, somewhere else. Increasingly, these "other people" who continue family farms, or preserve the land, or who hoe, or who have some kind of living spiritual life are far away indeed, perhaps for the majority to gawk at, like tourists on some distant continent. However, if the trees in Eden bear any living meaning for us today, we are the ones who have to realize it, make it real. And we can only do this with real trees, in actual dirt, in a world in which people get angry at one another, get callused hands, have to work through hard questions in solitude.

There is an old Hubbardston apple tree near the spring creek's path through our oldest orchard. There's nothing especially notable about it: its trunk gray, rough, its leaves that flat green, its apples hard, small, green, yet already blushing. But our knowing it is indivisible from its life: it lives, sap circulates like blood through its veins, out to its leaves' very extremities, and perhaps if we could see its awareness, this would extend around it in a kind of languorous halo, down into the earth and up into the air, a globe of tree-knowing nearly a century old. To know, in this sense, is to be aware, not just of ourselves but of others, even of trees and plants, which have their own knowing too.

On New Year's Day some years ago I spoke to the British poet Kathleen Raine, then in her eighties, who had just gotten a kitten, as I had just gotten a puppy. "You know," she said to me, "animals are not a substitute for human companionship—they're a whole different order." The same is true of plants, and I think that herein lies a mystery of orchard work that's not easily exhausted, perhaps a mystery that even goes to the heart of why we're here on earth, among other beings who aren't—I said, *aren't*—human. It's easy for us to project human qualities onto animals or even plants, but the mystery comes in when you realize that you're dealing with a consciousness that is different in kind from your own, indeed of a different order, with different faculties.

How did we come to be disjunct from these other consciousnesses? Why is there distress and suffering in this world where we find ourselves? Jakob Böhme, the great German visionary of the seventeenth century, and Louis-Claude de Saint-Martin, the great French theosopher of the eighteenth century, said that all nature bore the marks of some immense catastrophe, and that our purpose as humans is to redeem this disruption—whose fault, after all, is ours. We, Saint-Martin insisted, must be the repairers, those who redeem and reunite the various long-separated limbs of paradise. But in our day, not so far from his after all, we still see suffering in nature as in ourselves.

Occasionally, for instance, we'll be walking through the orchard, and notice that a certain tree looks a bit peaked. Perhaps it's mid-August, and admittedly there might be some disease going around—but this one doesn't just have slightly dulled leaves. Rather, there's something especially weak about it, something you notice as soon as you look at it. Why? What is it that separates this one tree from the others? Chances are that next spring, this same tree will be almost leafless, many of its limbs dried, and later that summer it will be dead. But the curious thing is, the other trees in that row will be flourishing, and so the question will linger in your mind as you fire up the chain saw and cut down that dead tree: How is it that life withdrew from this tree, almost as if life withdrew from it out into the others?

A tree is a living creature, and I have wondered sometimes if there is a tree consciousness, what in Greek mythology were called "dryads." Who is to say that trees have no consciousness? We modern humans judge all else by our own ratiocentrism, and fail to recognize that numerous kinds of consciousness can exist, that birds in a flock or bees in a hive might be united in ways we no longer see; or that plants in a field or orchard might communicate, sharing consciousness too. In ancient Asia and Europe, even minerals and water were seen as sentient—hence the oreads and naiads. But such views were mostly discarded with the so-called Enlightenment, and perhaps only when they are restored will we see the earth and our place on it aright once again.

For surely there are mysteries about the growth of trees. Once, some years ago, our family bought sixty-five acres of heavy clay farmland about ten miles away from our main farm, and planted it out in orchard, some 6,500 young trees in a sloping landscape that reminded me very much of the Great Plains, for when you stood on the highest part in the back ten acres, you felt almost as if you were encircled by the horizon. It was a landscape very different from our home farm, and I remember how cold and windy it was up there in the early spring. Truth is, the wind was always blowing out there, and even though it was only a short distance from terrain we were used to, it might as well have been in a different country entirely.

Now, I mention this place because it is alien to us; it was alien when we first went there, and it still is. We never made ourselves at home there; no one lived out there and cared for the place, and we didn't even really talk to our closest neighbors. I remember one sunny, hot July afternoon shortly after we had planted that orchard—which was laid out well, with blocks of different varieties set up for optimum pollination—when I was driving a tractor along the far northern slope nearest our neighbor's orchard. The farmer whose orchard adjoined ours there emerged from between two rows, driving an older, reddish-orange and gray tractor, behind it a small brush hog. He pulled up, stopped, shut his engine off, and pulled out his ear plugs.

"How's it going?" I asked.

"Not bad." He had a gray beard and his face was sun and windburned—crow's-feet when he smiled, and white teeth.

"You wear earplugs?" I was a little surprised.

"Since I lost my hearing in one ear on the spray rig." Spray rigs—big tanks on large, chest-high tires, mounted behind which is a fan that blows pesticides or fungicides clear through the trees—are loud, no doubt about that, especially because the tractor engine combines with the roar of the spray rig engine. They can be heard for miles, sometimes. It's a sound I grew up with, though I've never sprayed much myself.

We spoke for a while, and he told me, just in passing, that when he set out his orchard, he'd put in five or ten miles of drainage pipe.

"How much did you folks put in?" he asked, and gazed directly into my eyes.

"None yet."

"Be a good idea. This ground cracks like that," he indicated with a glance, "and it means the trees don't get water right. Get wet feet, and sometimes die out."

It was just a passing comment, part of a longer conversation, but I remember it so clearly because everything he said was prophetic. For the ground did indeed crack like that—the soil split into fissures around the saplings, and when it rained, the water wouldn't run off, but just pooled at the base of the trees, filling those fissures. This in turn created conditions perfect for what's called collar rot, and shortly some of our little trees looked weak. Many fought valiantly for life, but this only meant they stayed the same size they were when planted, and slowly they died. It took some years, but eventually the orchard looked spotty, here and there no trees at all, elsewhere broken rows that made spraying difficult. At first we hoped that some trees would die and the rest would flourish, but eventually we realized that, except for the high land to the northeast, the orchard just wouldn't ever be commercially successful.

Now, I mention this debacle because it exemplifies well enough why large-scale orchard farming, or large-scale farming of any kind, is fraught with danger. And that danger is, perhaps most of all, that one cannot offer sufficient attention to such an orchard. Someone has to live there; it has to be *cared* for. That orchard, I think, pined away. "Pined away" is an interesting phrase, capturing the way that pines die by turning brown, but having an emotional implication that, here, is especially appropriate. For an orchard requires you to pay attention to each individual tree, and to know the landscape and its needs. That's why corporate farming, in the end, will always be inappropriate to the land, because corporate farming has no culture; it grinds up and flattens, but it cannot love, and in the end, that is the most important element of all. However intangible love may seem, its presence is more tangible than anything else.

I have wondered whether its presence is tangible even in the wild, for instance among tamaracks. Our farm was once surrounded by tamaracks; they populated the swampland both north and south of the main house—indeed, on the oldest map of this area one sees only tamarack swamp marked. Those tamaracks died earlier in the twentieth century, their trunks standing like sentinels of a former time, long rotted and gone before my generation was born, and it's possible that they died not just from disease, but from deeper changes in the landscape, from the swamp's draining and all the human changes. For you can still find tamaracks in the north woods; they did not all die, only those in the south.

The tamarack is a strange kind of tree, like hemlock in its ethereal quality, but not so reclusive, for whereas hemlocks prefer northern slopes in the deep woods, tamaracks grow in and around marshes, and disrobe each autumn, losing their needles before winter. A hemlock is shy, while a tamarack is more forthright. It must have been a breathtaking, elegant sight when in the spring the tamaracks were all cloudy with new green needles, enveloping the straight brown trunks like a mysterious verdant fog over the brackish water and bracken.

Perhaps what appears to us as death from disease really comes from a withdrawal of the trees from the landscape, and perhaps for tamaracks to flourish again, there must be again the possibility that they *could* flourish; maybe the invisible tamaracks, seen in the mind's eye, have to be there first. But the whole landscape has changed, and the tamarack swamps are gone, replaced by poplar and elm and puckerbrush, or blueberries and cornfields, or ponds, and it is hard to envision the tamarack's return save as an occasional reminder, like acreage of unplowed prairie, of what once was here.

Yet my cousin Peter Joe and I have planted tamaracks, his around the pond below his house, mine near another pond near our swamp. A few died, but some have flourished, and now I scarcely believe it when I see those trees far taller than I am, feathery green needles and maroon young cones near the branchtips. It is true that the original tamaracks have died, but our new ones are doing well, breathtakingly tall and broad, there on the northwest corner of the pond, curtseying veiled green ladies. And we look at them in a different light than if they were common in these parts anymore. What has once died out and then been reborn you see anew, appreciative as a blind man restored to sight.

So it is too with elder varieties of apples. One can scarcely find an elder variety around: all the orchards have converted to Red Delicious, Yellow Delicious, Jonathans, Romes, and a few other kinds. I have nothing against these upstart apples, but it is foolish to discard the whole of antiquity, all those older apples, in favor of only the few most suitable for industrial production. To plant rare apples is to preserve the human inheritance. We need Hubbardstons and Wolf Rivers, Cox's Orange Pippins and Westfields, Snow and

Niger apples, William's Reds and Tolman Sweets, Winter Bananas and Spitzenburgs (Thomas Jefferson's favorite apple, which is good enough for me). How foolish that we, intoxicated by "progress," have nearly abandoned them all!

There are thousands of apple varieties, most of them not even available in the United States until recently, and each of them differs from the next as much as you differ from whoever is sitting nearest you: each apple variety has its own personality, hardiness, tendencies, special flavor. What's more, many of the older varieties have special characteristics that modern packagers don't seem to appreciate. Whereas a Delicious will turn mealy if left unrefrigerated, many of the older varieties actually grow sweeter and remain firm in storage: you can bury them for the winter, take them out in spring, and they will be better old than before. If you did that with any modern variety, you would remove it best from storage with a scraper and a sponge.

Actually, I have a theory about why certain varieties have become the standard. Sweetness is certainly one reason: many older varieties are tart. But it's more than that: If a bag of apples goes mealy, you have to throw them out and buy another. Like so many other modern practices, there's not much sense in this one. We moderns want the most disease-susceptible varieties in the world, which require the most pesticides, fungicides, and fertilizers, only to have the apples turn mealy in the refrigerator drawer—when all the time, farmers could be growing older or newer varieties that are disease-resistant, have unique flavors, and last much longer in the fridge. Why don't they? Industrialization, of course: big corporations want to sell bags of identical, disposable fruit. It might seem logical; it just doesn't make any sense.

This, of course, is the tree of knowledge of good and evil: the tree that we know for what it is, the gnarled old tree alongside the orchard whose fruit comes from another age entirely. Or the young trees that my father and I just planted, two rows of

Spitzenburgs and others, whose first harvest will take place in a few years, but whose fruit will taste the sweeter for knowing what it is, and that it has been nearly forgotten in the rush to make all our farms into factories. Like the tamaracks, these antique trees represent faith in the future, our statement that despite all the madness in the world, the earth will bring forth verdantly and in extravagant abundance.

Now we know, you see: we know that all we do represents the choice for good or for evil. Now we are all offered the necessity to choose, in full knowledge. We choose to be among the destroyers or among the preservers, among those who offer just inflated currency to our children's children, if that, or among those who offer the world, and all the trees of life in this erstwhile Eden whose abundance even in this fallen state is scarcely to be believed. We may choose to care for the earth and to help those who do so in our stead, or we may be among the unseeing hordes whose blind destruction fuels this consuming, feverish society. Each day, in small decisions, we incrementally decide the fate of this world—even as we hoe, and talk about original sin in humid July haze under a Michigan sun.

I suppose that it is dangerous, but I offer it nonetheless, a concluding parable that might be interpreted as having to do with spirituality. A man finds a magnificent tree growing in his garden. He didn't really cultivate the tree—at least, he can't remember cultivating it, but there it is nonetheless. The trouble comes when he concludes that since he didn't seem to have done much of anything to grow the tree (it was perhaps a tree he inherited from a previous owner), *no one* should do anything to cultivate such trees. So he goes about preaching to his neighbors that they are fools to water and tend their trees; after all, *his* just appeared in his garden, or so it seemed to him. And so many neighbors listen, and their garden trees wither for lack of water or fertilizer or good soil or adequate sun. What's more, when good gardeners come along, the neighbors won't listen, because everyone knows that such trees just grow on their own. And after all, sometimes they do seem to.

# Undermined by the Nothing

East and south of our farm are dense woods, cut with precipitous ravines and home to all manner of animals—sometimes even an occasional drifter who builds a makeshift shelter out there. You'll know he's there because there'll be a thin line of smoke rising from his camp, somewhere out in the sandy hills. The land, and this scene of a bearded hobo making camp, could belong to a century or two before. Why does this land, so close to a city, remain this wild? Surely, you would think, it's prime for so-called development, ready to host subdivisions and strip malls, pavement and litter, all the amenities of what we call civilization. But in fact these woods and open lands can't be built upon, for deep below the surface run plaster mines, invisible shafts following the gypsum lodes through the subterranean strata.

The undermined land, untamed and forested, is miles long and wide, populated by all manner of creatures. There's a certain irony in the fact that American industrialism, so intent on squeezing every last bit of money out of every bit of earth, is responsible for this refuge from citification, but I suppose one shouldn't inspect too closely where such a gift has come from. For the extraction of gypsum from under the surface has made of this land a strange and almost fantastic place, where great holes may open in the earth overnight, vast pits from the edge of which you can see the trees down below. The deer will avoid going down into some of them; you can see the deer trails through the brown oak leaves, weaving around the sinkholes, along the ridges.

These sinkholes can appear suddenly, anywhere that the mines have reached. The earth will look quite ordinary, just as it has any other day, trees as solid as yesterday, the soil as sandy, the leaves as green—and the next day everything will have shifted. You'll walk to the same place, stand there on a sunny summer afternoon, and with a furrowed brow, gaze penetratingly at the landscape, trying to see what has changed. And then you'll see that where yesterday was a sloping hill now is a concavity, all the trees suddenly sloping toward one another as though curtsying.

It seems to me that our whole world is like this, but we don't notice it, rarely recognizing the insubstantiality and transience of everything we see. It's just that here, life's sinkholes collapse more quickly, so you can see how things really are. My Uncle Dave tells the story of how, years ago, he cared for an orchard about two miles east of our farm. Caring for an orchard means that you trim the trees, spray them, keep the grass cut, and so forth. That orchard was, like ours, on a residential street, but it was set back from the road, and abutted the open land of the plaster mine company, so that you had there the three kinds of land: citified, agricultural, and wild. One morning my uncle drove the tractor and spray rig over there—and sat at the entrance road on his idling tractor, gazing at the great hole where the night before had been an orchard. You could still see the tops of some of the trees, when you walked closer to the hole's edge.

Now, to understand the full import of this story, it might be helpful to know that a spray rig—which rides on two shoulder-high fat tires—is full of water and fungicide or pesticide, so it weighs quite a bit, as of course does the bright green John Deere tractor that pulls it. You can imagine what would have happened had my uncle decided to spray that orchard the night before—

surely the equipment's weight would have triggered the collapse, for that night the mine had collapsed on its own. This is, I suppose, little different from dozens of other stories in which someone nearly escaped death—the lightning strike story comes to mind—but it illustrates better than most how a landscape, taken for granted, might nonetheless disappear without warning.

This undermining of the land, which began early in the twentieth century, has long struck me as richly symbolic, illustrative of original sin. Calvinism, drawing on Augustinian precedent, has traditionally held that mankind is fundamentally flawed, that sin is intrinsic to the present human condition. As the New England Primer once had it, "In Adam's Fall / We sinned all." Some claim that this is a peculiarly Christian idea and, further, that it is limited to Augustinian Western European Christianity, which is undoubtedly true if we are speaking about the specific concept of original sin. But there is within this idea more generally a profound insight, present in all the great religious traditions, that there's something fundamentally disjointed in contemporary modes of being, in our greedy, confused, frightened, angry little lives. Many, perhaps nearly all of us have great unseen caverns in our psyches, too, precariously held up by boards, catastrophes in the making.

Let me offer you an example, a story now legendary in our family. Before it collapsed into the earth and vanished from sight, this very same orchard was the scene of another calamity, perhaps what we could call a moral revelation. It seems that one autumn Sunday during the early 1960s, my grandparents came home from church as they always did, around noon, and my grandmother went about preparing Sunday dinner. After they had eaten, it was customary to take a nap, and so they did, but my grandfather was roused by a telephone call from a policeman, asking whether it was indeed true that we were giving away free apples to all takers at this orchard for which he and my uncle were responsible. "Of course not," he replied. "Then you'd better get over here," said the policeman.

When my grandfather arrived at the orchard, driving his round-fendered turquoise Buick, the scene that greeted him was rather startling. For there were automobiles of all descriptions out in the orchard—people who had driven across town, and from out of town, alerted to the "free apples" by our neighbors, many of whom had also come to take their share in the orchard. There were people carrying off paper bags and cartons and half bushels of apples; there were apples in trunks and in back seats, people perched in trees, matronly women parading by with children in tow, elderly men and paunchy middle-aged fathers with black-rimmed glasses—and two police cruisers, the officers drawn in by the traffic and commotion. They directed traffic.

Now, you must understand that many of these people were our suburban neighbors; they knew my family, knew my grandfather and my uncles and my father. They could have called—one of them could have called. Just one. But no one did. Instead, the rumor began that the apples were free, and spread like some virus, crackling along the telephone lines, drawing in complete strangers from far away, and everyone was willing to believe that we were giving away apples. Even as my grandfather stood there, a thick, bullnecked man, and charged people for what they were taking, still others managed to get away, and after it all was over, a few unclaimed bags and boxes remained there on the trampled grass.

I know few better examples of original sin. How else would you explain this? You know as well as I do that these folks were culpable—and that their guilt was like that of any mob, like that of Germans or Russians or Chinese or Americans or any people who, in a corrupt society, go along with events. People may know better, but once that fragile meniscus of conventional behavior is broken, why, the water flows out of its boundaries, the crowd rushes this way or that. Modern America is very much a herd society, I think, symbolized by a vast sea of sports fanatics in a stadium, and such a mob mentality is inherently corruptible. I like individuals, but I tend to dislike groups, and the larger the mob, the less I like it. The herd is rarely right.

Of course, my own sympathy for individuals extends so far that I cannot imagine a God who would condemn people to eternity in hell. In this respect, I am a bad Calvinist, I suppose, for though something like original sin is visible in human nature, it is hard for me to proceed from this to the condemnation of people to an eternal hell, making of God some cosmic warden. Surely hell is a function of our own ignorance and willful refusal to see God, and for us lasts only so long as is required for our error to be burned up, like fuel for flames. Naturally, some people seem to accumulate quite a supply of wood, so much that it might well seem like eternity, but in the end the confusion is burned up.

Yet when we turn to crowds, we're looking at another animal entirely. Evil is accomplished, in the modern era, by herds of people, shunted this way or that by apoplectic shouting tyrants or monstrous and sullen cold-eyed dictators whose power comes from herding with fear as their goad. Ours is the age of the masses—of that there can be no doubt—and I wonder whether we recognize how destructiveness pervades our era as a result. For it is one thing for us to condemn Nazi rallies long ago and far off, but quite another to realize that mass advertising, consumerism, mass tourism, mass transportation, mass communication, all work along fundamentally similar lines. Modernity spawns—modernity *is*—human herds that leave behind plenty of trampled, dead grass.

The grand delusion, of course, is that we are not individually culpable if we acquiesce in mass destruction. We demonize the Germans under Hitler, the Russians under Stalin, failing to recognize that the modern era is all of a piece, and that we are at this very moment contributing to the destruction of the natural world, unthinkingly acquiescing in a juggernaut that leaves behind a cracked, dead land. But the consequences of what we do are often hidden from us by our machinery and our entertaining distractions, our moving picture shows whose glamorous images glow in the darkness of a theater, even a theater in a foul and inhuman slum across whose barren pavement discarded plastic skitters and lodges against a rusting fence. We see the moving picture show; we ignore the tenements and the degradation. We participate in the machine, and, becoming one of the crowd, we fail to see where we really are.

Perhaps most alarming isn't the growing abyss between the countless poor and the enormously rich elite, but that they are both ruled by herd mentalities, and that underneath the latest fashion, the latest form of gang lingo or flashy shoes, is nothing at all, no culture, no context, the Nothing. Just air. At any moment the apparently solid earth might fall away, the projector stop, and the bedazzled crowd stand, suddenly bewildered as the spell evaporates and everyone again becomes an individual, puzzled that he was ever whipped up into such a frenzy over nothing. For of course the greatest triumph of delusion is to make the countless poor cheer on the rich, to make the hopeless masses appear to participate by machinery in the worlds of power and greed. But when it is all over, everyone must stand again an individual, on trampled grass, near discarded paper and other residue of fleeting, deluded enthusiasms. The rich and the poor alike stand alone amid the trash of their lives.

What is the Nothing? It is what's left when consumerist illusions disappear, when the electricity goes off, when the whirring machinery stops. For we can distract ourselves with all kinds of sophisticated dog-and-pony shows, but beyond the shows is no culture, nothing that reveals the meaning of this cottage or that apple tree, this jug, that dog, this blade of grass. Schoolchildren know the Nothing intimately; in school they grow accustomed to it, acclimated to living in a press of people thronging among lighted billboards advertising trinkets, to valuing what their neighbors think, to longing for the latest fashion, to social regimentation and cheering crowds, from which the only respite is that group of renegade outsiders whose faux resistance is but joining another herd, and underneath whose resistance is, of course, the Nothing.

This is why the farm is so profoundly significant: it represents specific things, particular trees, a particular kind of sandy soil, a hawk, a deer, an owl, a fox, an antiquated red tractor, an old, thick-boarded red barn, a boulder on which you've sat a thousand times. These are not the Nothing. They are, in fact, like the people who farm the land—Peter Joseph, Nathan, Jim, Dave— emphatically real, alive, and bearing in themselves a certain kind of knowledge that accrues by being. Ah, you say, people I will accept, but a hawk, a boulder, a barn, a battered red Farmall tractor, these can't *know*, can they? Yet perhaps there is a kind of knowing in all things that are known and loved for what they are, and from this mutual knowing arises meaning. In their thingness, in their being, everything here gainsays the Nothing. As you move, they register your movement like a faithful dog.

But of course, how much money is meaning or love worth? When you sell a field to a "developer" and he "develops" it by ripping up the earth, covering it with pavement, making it just another site for a strip mall, your income is of a wholly different sort: you have diminished the incalculable into the merely quantified. Memories, meanings, the fruitful earth, these do not have a monetary value, and when we reduce what surrounds us to that most vulgar of levels, what is left? This is what I mean by "the Nothing," a term for the blankness, the absence of vitality, the meaninglessness that infects modern life like some invisible plague, whose blankness is behind all those dots on your screen, behind all the ads and the envy. Soul sold for less than a mess of pottage.

My family has not sold our mineral rights to the miners or exploiters, though needless to say, the lure is always there, the siren call is always present, and there is virtually no support in modern society for the farm's preservation. Indeed, quite the opposite: for more than a century, America has denigrated farmers, and valued the exploiter, the one who makes a quick buck on the fast turnover, the guy with a Cadillac, a paunch, and an ingratiating, false smile. What's worse, we cannot quantify what the land means, we cannot say that this or that parcel produces less meaning per acre. Of course, our land is not infertile: high and well drained, it is some of the richest, best apple, peach, and sweet corn ground in America. But even so, the oily realtors circle, the taxes rise, and the prices for crops keep dropping.

What is this strange sleight of hand that so easily deceives us into valuing the fleeting, discardable, and meaningless over the perennial, fruitful, and meaningful? Surely it is a peculiar affair that deserves investigation. Perhaps strangest of all: when you bring this subject up in mixed company, inevitably many people will agree with you, even though society en masse continues on this very same course, away from the land, away from what matters, toward the ephemeral. It is as though vast crowds had somehow gotten entranced by some will-o'-the-wisp, and left everything to go traipsing over acres of pavement, running and staggering day and night through an alien land after an illuminated neon Nothing.

Because I live on a farm, I write about a farm, but these ideas have wider application. If no man is an island, neither is a farm, for what happens to this one place has countless unseen ramifications; it does not stand alone. Any open land, any woods, any place beloved by someone, is under the same threat. If we cannot acknowledge that there are higher values than the merely monetary, then the danger and destruction can only increase as the tide of people grows ever greater. What happened in that little orchard we once cared for—its plunder by strangers, its collapse into the abyss—can happen anywhere nowadays. The original sin is not greed, but forgetting and ignoring our real purpose on earth.

I well remember the first time I read those remarkable lines of Rilke, who, in his letters to his publisher, Anton Kippenberg, wrote at length about this destruction modernity was wreaking upon the world, and insisted that we were nonetheless the "bees of the invisible," the "transmuters of the world," whose purpose was to transform by imagination all the things that we love, bring them forth in the invisible. For his grandparents, he said, a house, a well, a coat, these things meant infinitely more than they mean to his generation. And today from America there come facsimile-things—an American house, an American apple has *nothing* in common with the house or fruit of our forefathers. "We are," he added, "perhaps the last to have still known such things." But he was not despairing, because these beloved things must now, he said, be transmuted into the invisible.

Perhaps this conviction of Rilke's reflects the reversal of original sin, human history bracketed by the fall of humanity at its beginning and by the restitution of all things at its end. For if original sin has its manifestations in the destructiveness of modernity, still, seeded throughout this era are the kernels of another, of a turning-about and a restoring. In the works of great poets and great artists, we see just such a transmutation, transferring the fleeting things of this world into consciousness, describing and depicting, bringing the visible into the invisible. And perhaps all great artists and writers are but forerunners of some as yet unrecognized momentous transforming, a bringing-forth into paradise, not just of our little selves, but of all that and whom we love.

Those who seek to gain the world do indeed lose their souls. To those who have the invisible riches of the soul, more shall be given, but to those who have not, even that which they have will be taken away. I have known more than one man and woman obsessed with accumulation of wealth or power, and it is a peculiar thing how they become self-caricatures as time goes on, turning into a shell, a collection of personality tics and petty grudges, sinking into a morass of conniving, lying, and fear. Even as they gain political power or wealth, they lose who they are and sink down into selfish conspiring. The path downward means ceasing to love or care about anything but one's self and is a sinking below the human; the path upward is a flowering of love for one's place and people that culminates in transcending them—it is a rising above the human.

For what if life were utterly different than we have been taught? What if its meanings were to be found not in profit, but in love? And what if, after we died, what we inherited corresponded only and exactly to what we had transmuted by pure, unattached love in this world? What if we were each called to be messiahs of nature and of one another? Surely we are called to a vocation higher than getting and spending—we know that this is so, for we are each faced by death, who makes a mockery of all our acquisitions, sweeps them away in an instant. To become who we truly are, we must begin where we are, in this moment, transient beings in a fragile world, travelers whose only memento, in the end, is love or its absence.

# No Man's Land

The abandoned orchard stands not far from where I write, a dense tangle of tall, dark suckers that clatter together in the winter wind, festooned with wild grapevines and poison ivy now desiccated by the cold. I remember when the old man who used to live there still tended the land, though in those days he was already too old to do it well, too stiff and bent to trim the trees even then. Sometimes you glimpse deer browsing through the leaves with tentative nibbles, glancing up through the brush at you, startled that there's a human presence here. Increasingly, it's hard to walk through the tangle of puckerbrush that's grown up, and soon the woods will begin to reclaim its own. This is certainly no man's land, now.

The question is what will become of it. Because whereas in Europe or England people have a respect for the land as it is, in America people have no such respect. I do not think Americans have ever come to terms with the earth on which they live, any more than they have come to terms with the land's original inhabitants. Whereas Christians in Europe drew upon and incorporated "pagan" understanding of the land and sacred places, America was built with a willful disregard for any such considerations. Our churches are built any old place, not on prior native sacred sites as in Europe, and there is in this a profound symbolism (or lack thereof). In America, not only do most people not care about the land's meaning or preservation, in fact most people argue violently in favor of doing anything you please with it.

Now, this land I'm talking about is good, high, well-drained orchard land, and there are not many such places in this world. It is a rare thing, but it requires someone to work it. An orchard does not grow by itself: it requires human hands to tame and care for it. And this is where the problem comes in, because not only are there not so many such places in this world, there are also not so many people who know how to care for them. When the old farmer died, he left only one child, a daughter who had married a city man and had moved to a suburb outside Chicago. Like many who grew up on farms and left them in the middle of the twentieth century, she disliked what the farm meant: for her, it meant the drudgery her mother and father had endured, and little else.

So the land sat idle. Occasionally I would walk it with my dog, cast an eye to its slopes, and thought of what it would look like with neat rows of young trees, perhaps old varieties like Bananas or Hubbardstons, Westfields or even dinner-plate-sized Wolf Rivers. My dog liked the land, for in it you could scare up a rabbit or some other critter every few feet, and there were all sorts of interesting scents there, so the dog reliably informed me. There is something bittersweet about an abandoned farm: walking it, you're truly walking on the border between the wild and the domesticated. In it is something akin to the dog, who also lives on precisely this borderland, ready to curl up at your feet, but ready also to bay at the moon and rip the throat from a rabbit or woodchuck.

An abandoned orchard does not easily turn to wilderness, for however long the apple trees stand, there is evidence of domestication, reminders of human presence like those flowers one finds blooming at the site of a homestead abandoned and obliterated decades before. Apple trees retain their shape, their main trimmed limbs, even after many years, even after around them scrub oak and maple and poplar have grown high, even after they stand like sentinels from another era in the midst of a woods, among brown leaves—so long as the fruit trees remain, you can make out where the orchard was. Indeed, several miles to the east of our farm, when I was young I found on a hill above the river valley some ancient plum trees in a circle—and later discovered that they may well have been tended by Indians more than three-quarters of a century before, having marked a sacred place.

Walking through this abandoned orchard now, though, I see no sign of sacred plum trees in a circle, only the more mundane rows of a Dutch farmer, and the occasional piece of rusting equipment embedded in soil and brown, rustling grass and weeds. Some of the equipment belongs to another time entirely, when he must have farmed with horses: here is an ancient plow, from which the rust falls in large dark flakes when you push it with your foot, experimentally. And here what looks to be a potato planter, farther on a hay rake, its large curving tines pitted and reddish-brown. None of them can move, for the soil is rising slowly, year by year, inexorably covering them until they are like the ruins of Nineveh. They belong to a world as nearly distant, I think.

When we walk only a bit further, we find ourselves amid the carefully tended, unnaturally green lawns of a condominium complex, as forbidding and silent as an abandoned city. The ambience is rather like that of an abandoned desert village on a high mesa, where the last human dweller left more than a thousand years ago. People live here, more or less, but there is no trace of them in the way that a farmer leaves traces, by shaping and working with his world—rather, this is a nearly artificial realm, and I would not be surprised if those bright green decorative bushes atop piles of wood chips were made of plastic so as to be less trouble. The heating units hum in the early winter air. The dog noses alongside one of the buildings, but returns to the woods with a certain noticeable gladness.

It surprises me to find woods like these so close to the city. If you listen closely, you can hear the rush of traffic, until you

137

descend into the stillness of the ravines. The woods then close around you as you descend, the sides of your boots digging into the steep, oak-leaf-covered slope, the dog padding through the leaves ahead of you. If, as Lao Tsu wrote, all things emerge from the great valley, the Mother, then what is it that happens when we descend back into the ravine? Places like this remain alive because they cannot easily be exploited; wooded ravines separate us from the harried and destructive noisy human world with each step we take into them. Here is a preternatural enveloping silence, in which the occasional chickadee's voice appears only briefly, an inconstant soloist, the earth's dark moistness around us now.

Down below is a thin clear stream whose origin is the earth itself, pulsing currents of water that never cease, but run silently down the slopes to this rivulet. Artesian springs well up all along these slopes, and we must walk carefully to avoid a boot submerged in that saturated muck marking their presence. You can see where, in the spring, the skunk cabbage will spread its wings and open to the pale sun filtering through the oak and maple limbs, and where the raccoon and fox and deer have left their telltale footprints, their signatures in the soft earth. Along the narrow stream below, deer tracks mark where they have watered, and where they bounded up the far side of the ravine along a trail barely visible that opens into the abandoned orchard and its fallen apples, a delicacy to the wintering deer.

We too emerge from the woods into the white light of a cloudy winter day, as if the sun could be anywhere overhead, or perhaps was lost or had departed, leaving behind only a uniform light like that of fluorescent bulbs. My dog is happy to be in the orchard again, full of that explosive delight a dog has when leaping into that boundary between wilderness and domestication, where it truly belongs. Already we can see ahead what remains of the old barn and house, the gray planks that have seen too many winters already, have reached indeed their own winter. Here they must have had a garden, there the cattle must have grazed, and along the orchard must have been a long field, now punctuated by brushy spires and brambles.

As we stand near the ruins of the house and barn and my dog prowls, sniffing delicately at more than a century of lives now vanished, I wonder at how quickly a way of life can become extinct. Only a few decades before, people farmed with horses and still retained something of the wisdom that joins this world and the invisible, but it is as if by some mass fascination, America has abruptly forgotten everything, intoxicated by the ecstasy of selling its soul to the devil for a pittance. How thoroughly Hamilton won and Jefferson lost in the battle between mercantilism and agrarianism is nowhere better illustrated than here, amid the debris and weeds where once was a well-run family farm.

The barn was a good one, built from shaved timbers whose length makes me think at once of the labors required in putting together such a building. It wasn't a huge barn, like some, but it was an old one: on some of the timbers there is bark that has seen more than a hundred summers. I have never been to a community barn-raising, for when I was growing up we had all the barns we needed, and put up pole barns of sheet metal and two-by-four struts when our oldest one burned down, struck by lightning several decades ago. But it must have been a remarkable sight, all those farm men out lifting and positioning, shouting and pointing, shaving down beams and hammering on the sideboards. Such a thing isn't possible nowadays: if you wanted to host a barn-raising, whom would you call?

Anyway, this old barn has seen its demise, for now broken boards protrude through tufts of brown grass, and much of it is burned, flames quenched in the end by rain to leave behind these charred and shattered remains. Here, where the cattle must have come in, you can see the runners of a small sleigh and its leather seat flanked by a small metal ridge for little hands to clutch when the horse trotted faster through the snow. When did a man drive this sleigh through the woods to town with bundled children beside him? Was it a century ago already? The man, the woods, the farm, and even the village are long gone, irretrievably gone, as surely as if we had fought a war against our own history, and won, vanquishing ourselves.

There is a story in the debris. Outside what remains of the house are a few thick-rimmed ceramic crocks, lined with moss. In one of them is a rusted muffin tin, and I think of the warm and steaming muffins once baked in this farm kitchen, of the green pickles steeping in the crocks. Here lies the paraphernalia of a kitchen past, a modest kitchen; you can see where the farm wife walked from the house to the fruit cellar underneath the shed: the door still swings on rusted hinges beneath a carefully tapered entrance. Above, inside the shed between whose slats you can see sky, is a pair of gray, ancient crutches, one leaning against the ribbed wall beside a piece of cracked harness. That couple lived here until they died; he lived here even when he couldn't farm and couldn't walk, and after he was gone she lived on alone while the grass and the trees grew season by season. Are there ghosts in such a place, shades of the departed? How could there not be?

It was not an easy life for either of them, nor did they become rich. Their main satisfactions were small ones but tangible, like the view out back and east where the well-tended fence ran and the pasture, the neat barn and the couple of cows, the orchard off to one side with its tall and stately trees. The vegetables in summer and the fruit brought from the cellar in late winter, the clean and warm kitchen with its broad woodstove. They were simple people who didn't read or write, but they owned the land and house and barn, and they were free. A hard life, but a good one, and it was etched into their faces and lives indelibly, in the certainty of his walk, in the way they carried themselves. This was their place, and you could still see where the bulb flowers grew and blossomed whitely in spring. The flowers had already seen their last spring.

All over America are such farmhouse ruins. Often the farmsteads still stand, vacant and gaping, empty eyes and open door gazing out at a world that has forgotten them with an uncivil abruptness. A fine photographic essay might record these loneliest of places, once beloved and now unseemly and unkempt, noble and gray like an aristocrat gone to seed. But modern American society has no use for peasants or nobles: they get in the way of all our machinery, and their homesteads are only picturesque reminders that probably make us uneasy. We value the crass, the garish, and the superficial; we have long forgotten the wisdom of conserving and do not even know anymore what matters or why. Instead of a heart there is a hole; instead of a soul there is nothing at all; and a cold wind blows through the ruins of all that we leave behind.

As we leave the abandoned orchard and cross the road, we pass a small realtor's sign, upon which is perched a square red addition: SOLD. I heard about the sale in the usual way, over a cup of coffee at the local coffee shop. Apparently a development corporation from the outskirts of Detroit had bought the land and were planning on building a high-density subdivision there, or perhaps a subdivision with some convenience stores and a strip mall if they could get the right zoning changes. It is strange to think that some paunchy, jowly fellow behind a desk in some distant place had control of this land and, by extension, of our whole local economy of place, without ever having seen it or set foot on the ground. To him it was just a commodity, like pork bellies or widgets, abstract and without meaning. Just business.

We could discuss it in his office or in the coffee shop, but I doubt he'd ever know what I was talking about were I to say that the land was once a well-cared-for farm and ought to be again. No, he'd say, the market has to determine everything, and if you can't make money farming, then the land should be turned to another use. And it's all the same, it's all just use—the earth was given to man to use, and it makes no real difference whether it's used for a farm, or a subdivision, or a strip mall, or a strip mine. He might even throw in a bit of religion, and tell me that God planned it this way for our benefit, or a bit of propaganda, and say that this was progress and for the best. And anything I said about caring for the land or about community or family or agriculture being informed by spirituality—anything I said would disappear into the vacuum where his soul once was.

All across America are the same shoddily built buildings, the same haphazard commercial strips with clotted traffic, the same garish appliance stores and the same gaudy plastic fast food joints, while nearby a town languishes and dies, and farmland disappears. In Europe it is still different; in Europe when you leave a village or a city, you know it, and pass suddenly into open farmland whose contours have changed little in more than a thousand years. I think that Europeans have had a greater awareness of and respect for land than unrooted Americans, for European and English lands are informed by the ancient merging of pagan and Christian that is marked by the building of cathedrals upon sacred sites. In America we have yet to recognize anywhere as sacred earth.

From the beginning, Americans have had a casual disregard for the land. Perhaps this disrespect comes in part from America's vastness and the way it was settled in waves that lapped further west. Whenever settlers felt it necessary, they moved on, and always there was a frontier, a borderland between domestication and wilderness. Indeed, America was built by people who had separated from their families and homelands, sometimes two or three times removed, first by an ocean, then by subsequent moves inland. In this sense, it is comprehensible why even to this day Americans mostly have no real homeland in their own country and why the whole country is a thoughtless hodgepodge without rhyme or reason: rarely if ever in America does one find the continuity over generations and the harmony between man and nature that European inheritance and tradition have provided.

One might think that over time, Americans would come to terms with the land and truly settle down. But in fact this peculiar American fever to always be moving and building and tearing down grows even more intense. Families do not occupy the same land for generations—indeed, many families don't even remain families nowadays, much less pass on a sense of generational responsibility for and harmony with particular land. Everywhere swarm realtors and so-called developers: open land is called vacant, as though it is only crowned when there is a cheaply built convenience store upon it. And all across the country, everywhere you go, are new malls and new subdivisions, sucking the life from nearby cities and towns, only to themselves be abandoned in favor of some other mall or subdivision. It is a plague.

I think that our societal collapse has its origin in American rootlessness and in the notion that the individual property owner has no greater responsibility than to himself and his own immediate profit. The foundation of a stable society is in the land; the measure of a society is how it preserves and augments the land. Some people need cities, belong in cities, and I would not deny that. A living city has its own beauty, and complements the surrounding countryside. But American society has produced decaying, unlivable cities surrounded by isolated exurbs, and allows for no true countryside. Why? Because it's every man for himself, and no one is lauded for preserving what has come from the past. A people hellbent on extracting profit have not long until they, seeking riches, drag themselves into poverty.

The writing is on the wall. An acquaintance of mine was traveling in South America and witnessed there the poverty and degradation of people who only a few decades before lived with traditional dignity in rural lands, but now were driven to cities where they could neither work nor feed themselves. "You see this?" said a policeman to my acquaintance. "Here you see Chicago and Detroit in years to come. The same forces are at work all over the world." It is easy for us to fool ourselves into thinking that we have reached the end of history, that we are the only civilization never to fall. But without transportation on a vast scale, think of what would happen in the large cities, where people have long since forgotten where food comes from and have no local farms to provide it.

In the long run, a civilization can do nothing more damaging than to abandon its local farmland and come to rely on distant sources. It makes no sense whatever to make our Michigan city, surrounded as it is (or rather, was) by the finest orchard land in the Midwest, dependent on New Zealand or totalitarian China for its apples. Yet such are the forces at work today. It is madness, and will show itself so in the end. While today's skewed economy may make it seem efficient to fly or truck or ship food from the far ends of the earth, one day we will again need local farmers—and the land will not be there. Or perhaps we will see the desperate tearing down of houses and strip malls, slow and expensive efforts to restore what greed had stolen.

Let me offer another striking example of shortsightedness. Not far north of our farm, the last working farm within the Grand Rapids city limits, are rolling fields and orchards that mark the region known as Fruit Ridge. The Ridge runs for some miles, and is high, well-drained, fertile soil, perfect for apples; it is the single most concentrated and richest large region of orchard land in Michigan. But because apple prices have consistently been lower than the cost of growing, due to our bizarre "free trade" laws, farmers have only barely been able to hang on for another year. Surely it would make sense to preserve such land, which cannot be replaced—you cannot just put an orchard anywhere. Of course, lulled by cheap fruit imported from South America or elsewhere, most people don't notice the loss of such land, and the greedy are all too ready to make a quick buck.

In the meantime, a development corporation based in a distant big city pinpointed just this area for one of the largest shopping malls in the state. Never mind that there are already six large shopping malls in the metropolitan area, and that five of them are losing money and stores, one standing nearly empty, grass growing in its parking lot. Never mind that the proposed site is on a two-lane road; never mind that it is agricultural ground currently farmed; never mind that the only justification for building is short-term gain without the slightest consideration for proper land use, local residents, agricultural preservation, or the community as a whole. The corporation wants to spend a hundred million dollars to ruin an agricultural area, and the city lapdogs come running, for they have been in heat for years.

Ah, the city officials reply but, the city needs tax dollars; the city needs "progress" and "development." One would believe this if one didn't know that the city was awash in money already; if one didn't know that the same city builds sidewalks past open land and pays nearly a million dollars for a few acres to get rid of the excess money it already has; if one didn't know that the city's "progress" has already led inevitably to traffic, noise, pollution, overcrowding, crime, and the destruction of prime farmland. Facts are inconvenient things easily disposed of, evidently, if they get in the way of "progress." The mall was narrowly defeated by local residents despite the efforts of city officials and the corporation, who have promised to try again until they succeed. And so it goes. These events and many others flood by as I pass the realtor's sign and walk on home.

And it is not many weeks—early spring—before I hear the sound of bulldozers and heavy equipment. I drive by with my dog sitting in the passenger seat, as she is wont to do if I let her, gazing regally out at the passing world. The trees are just at the point of leafing out, but under the gray sky you can hardly tell. Half the orchard is already torn asunder, trees lying in piles with their tangled roots exposed, two huge bulldozers at work atop the brownish loam. We stop, and I step out; we stand at the edge of what once was the orchard, not far from the house and barn, but already there is no sign of all that we had passed through not long before.

There could be no more conclusive proof that beneath the apparent order of our suburban homes with their tidy mowed lawns is a profound disorder. To make a subdivision here is to do violence to the earth and to destroy the gentle harmony possible in a farm; those sidewalks and sealed houses are built upon a whirlwind's wreckage. And yet there's money to be made, so people make it. This is, as they say, the bottom line, and bottom it surely is. Yet curiously I feel little beyond a sense of sadness and loss; it is hard to be angry, any more than one could be angry at the wreckage left by a war: inflamed by something incomprehensible, they know not what they do. The dog's nose steams the truck window with a silvery aureole. Black-masked, she watches intently as nature is nailed to a cross.

Traditionally, orchards symbolize paradise. The ideal orchard requires no care, no sweat, no labor: fruit grows ripe and falls into your hand of its own accord, rows of verdant trees perpetually blooming and bearing. Such images appear in all the great traditions and resonate in our deepest longings: our longing for joy and true community, our longing for harmony with nature, our longing for being reconciled again with the divine. Even if all that we do is at odds with such images, even if our entire life seems a repudiation of such yearnings, still deep within us we harbor them. Perhaps all true literature, all poetry and art, reveal our lost paradise either as celebration or as lament.

But in this mutable world, few of us are granted entry into paradise; most of us willingly live in a no-man's-land. What bothers me most is not that people would choose the Nothing, but that

146

we have developed a society opposed to the very idea that there could be any other way of seeing the world, opposed by default to those who would preserve the deep relation between man, nature, and the divine symbolized in the images of paradise, a society that not only chooses the Nothing, but would have the rest of us choose it too. Surveying the wreckage of this old farm, I know what its replacement will look like: building after building sealed from the outside world, inhabitants who almost never set foot outside save perhaps to mow the lawn, or to go into the convenience store, gas station, office, or grocery. There will be no there there. Even memory of the farm will slowly vanish. And when they are called to account, they will say "I knew it not; I lived in no-man's-land." And that will be the truth.

# Words, Soil, Plants

Perhaps the salient thing about writing, in the end, is what one has to leave out, rather than what one actually writes. For every piece of writing ultimately is only a shell that one as a writer, like a hermit crab, abandons, so that it may be reinhabited by a reader who one day discovers it and scuttles inside to live there for a while. Writers rarely think about how a written work requires a reader to bring it to life, yet the life of a work comes not from a series of identical reactions, but rather out of a vast range of new interpretations, like generations of farmers inhabiting the same acreage and adapting it to new ways while maintaining the old.

I've often thought that writing is deeply analogous to farming, and so it is something of a comfort to find that insightful farmer of more than two centuries past, Crèvecoeur, remarking that words, like men, arise from a particular soil, and thrive when conditions are right. One could make too much of conditions, blaming them for the failure of another crop when in truth it was our own failure to adapt to them, to a drought with irrigation, to rain with proper drainage.

This analogy between writing and farming runs deeper than we might at first think. Both create something that wasn't there before: the writer, intellectual nourishment, and the farmer, physical. And both live in a different economy than the industrial, for both are primary creators, and do their work for love. The author creates the primary work, but in the industrial economy it must be "produced" and "marketed," and those who do this work, the fleet of merchants and sellers of every stripe, each adds his charges so that the writer experiences something much like the farmer whose bushel of wheat, sold for a dollar, is processed into the airy contents of countless bright boxes.

Here I am excluding the vast hordes of scribblers who produce the great piles of empty pages that clog our bookstores and obscure by their meaningless variety the genuinely meaningful books. How few are the books worth reading, and how true Emerson's rule that one ought to give a book a decade or more before deciding whether to read it. In our age of instantaneous consumption and disposal, there is in this rejection of the moment's fashion something salutary, perhaps even essential to health.

It may be that new times require new kinds of writing, and that our era and its technologies will demand and produce them. But increasingly I find myself dwelling not among the fashionable so much as among the ancients, those whose works have the patina of generations thumbing through them, and finding a particular quotation that speaks to this moment. Some nowadays claim that they do not want to be hampered by the shaping hand of an artist; they extol the delights of leaping from one collection of data to another, or of freeing readers to create their own texts. All this is well enough for some, I suppose, but I should much prefer, for my part, a work that has lived in the lives of a dozen or a thousand generations.

To me, a fine book is like an apple tree, whose present form comes from years of shaping, from the work of human eyes and hands informed by generations of experience and even, perhaps, by wisdom. Not for me the distorted, disjointed, frenetic, hyperbolic or nihilistic. A great book becomes so only via great readers, who recognize what it is, who hold it dear, whose repeated readings slowly unveil its deeper meanings. Over time, in fact, a work can acquire a whole new ambience, begin to develop around it elaborations and accretions, expanding, like branches spreading. Plato's dialogues come to mind—how much has been attributed to Plato, how much written about "what Plato thought," when of course what we have in the dialogues is never Plato himself. "Plato's thought," Middle Platonism, Neoplatonism, Renaissance Platonism, all these are the artfully trimmed, ever growing branches.

It's obvious enough that a plant grows in soil, but these days it seems increasingly common to try and forget this, in literature as in agriculture. Just as we have hydroponic agriculture, and evidently aim one day for synthetic *everything* emerging from some "replicator," so too we increasingly have hydroponic literature grown under artificial lights, using distilled water and scientifically formulated fertilizer. What other than hydroponic literature could we call some of the bizarre experiments published in the last quarter or half century, these strange anemic specimens that bear no trace of sunlight, have never felt the wind or clenched the dirt? These works begin and end nowhere; they reflect emptiness at an empty people.

What a mystery there is in rich soil! There's not a scientist alive who could by calculation or experimentation unveil the mysteries hidden in the soil's alchemy. We know by intricate analysis that the finest soil, rich and well drained like ours, gives to plants certain minerals and trace nutrients whose significance no one really knows. And even were we to bring all our formidable analytical machinery to bear upon it, the soil would never finally give up its secrets: it could not, for these secrets are bound up with the rain, the wind, the snow, the animals and the birds. We would be wise to ask Orpheus or Hermes what this means, but a child could tell us that newly turned soil in the spring has a rich and musty scent like a trunk rarely opened in a thousand years.

I doubt that there was ever a farmer who didn't inwardly marvel at this scent, delighting in it more than any other. A friend tells me that his father was plowing a field several springs past, and my friend's uncle stopped alongside the field's edge to watch, leaning against his pickup, his hands thrust into the side pockets of his worn blue overalls. Eventually my friend's father, then eighty years old, slowed, stopped, and shut off the tractor, glancing over at his brother with a sharp eye. "Going in a low gear," said his brother. "I like to watch it turn," said my friend's father, his gravelly voice informed by a lifetime of doing just that. I like to watch it turn: there's more in that laconic statement than meets the ear.

It is strange how many kinds of soil there are on our farm: each slope and incline has its own personality, and what here may be clay, there may be sand, there might be a loam, and but a few steps further, a dark black peat moss. We do have peat moss swamps on the farm, though they are not what they once were, for of course they have been drained for more than half a century. When my father was young, the peat caught fire and burned all summer, smoldering away down to the north and west, thin columns of black smoke rising day and night for months from subterranean flames until finally autumn rains put them out. Yet a hundred yards from the swamp, such a fire would be impossible, for the soil is abruptly clay, an oily gray more suitable for pottery than crops. But on the highlands and ridges is remarkable soil, which holds water even during droughts, yet the trees never drown or die of "wet feet."

It is strange, too, that as I write this I can visit this soil in my mind's eye—I could do so from the far side of the globe. Images arise in my mind of each piece of ground, of how the grass grows upon it, and what kind, where long saw-sharp swamp grass grows and where thin spears of orchard grass, where the soil is brown, where it is gray, and where it is black, how it changes as you walk up a ridge from west to east. Where the drains are, beneath the earth, and how they run; where the kildeer have their nest and from what direction the kildeer mother will raise an alarm from the field; in what hayfield the duck will often lay her eggs, and where; how the earth smells in the morning when it's been newly turned. Land over which you've walked incalculable times becomes a part of you, just as, in the end, you become a part of it.

And is this not also true of books? I think that we moderns are as uncomfortable with dirt as we are with our predecessors: we don't want to recognize that plants grow in soil, and books grow from the rich soil of other books. Not long ago, someone brought me a collection of poems written by a young woman who scorned literature—she wanted to write afresh, without being influenced by anyone. I could barely endure reading a selection, and returned them without comment, for they weren't poems, they were what someone who'd never read a poem thought poetry must be. This is what *sophomoric* really means, and it is a malady afflicting more than just sophomores. Just as many people forget that the food in the supermarket is grown in dirt, so many believe that literature can appear ex nihilo.

Indeed, dirt has become a bad word, signifying filth that we ought to avoid, that we ought to "progress beyond." This same blind faith in Progress is also responsible for the habitual modern denigration of the past: Who needs to know about the ancients, for have we not long since superseded them? They all lived in some dark age, whereas we are enlightened by someone else's invention of machinery. And so we have the peculiar modern phenomenon of writers who believe that they have superseded the past, that literature can exist without prior literature like some rootless plant growing in midair.

But I would like to celebrate dirt for a moment. Great literature draws on many sources—it springs up from emotional waters, glitters in the light of the intellectual sun, lives in the lives of people; it is the gift of a reader to other readers, of the spirit to the spirit. The richest writing grows only in soil made black and fertile by millennia of tradition, and though it appears as fresh and new as if it had just emerged from the earth, it can do so only by emerging from a mother tongue whose countless speakers all have contributed to it, given it life. Great literature is alive, is indeed filled with life, imbued by something beyond the individual poet or writer, who is like the waters across which the spirit moves and leaves its traces for us all to see.

Great literature speaks to the age in which it was created, but though its immediacy may seem to fade with time, it enriches its mother tongue and all those who enter its sphere. Upon how many works have Dante's or Shakespeare's enlivening touch fallen, how many were enriched by them, and could only be conceived as growing in a soil to which Dante or Shakespeare has contributed? Literary genius consists, certainly not in being able to catalogue everything ever written, but rather in the ability to manifest some new work that emerges from what has been written and said before, and that one day will in turn enrich some future work. Every great work is more a gift to the future than to the present; it is an act of faith.

So it is with farming, and with any work truly worth doing: it is a covenant with those to come. When John Taylor of Caroline County, Virginia, devoted many pages of his book *Arator* (1813) to manure, on its importance and ways to spread it on fields, many readers thought him tedious. But the truth is, he elaborates a subject of enormous import for the soil's preservation and enrichment. It is possible—as too many modern farmers have demonstrated—to farm without manure and to deplete the soil until it resembles a cracked desert, but such ways are a breach of faith with those to come.

Bad literature, popular literature, all the richness of colorful, vulgar speech, this is the manure out of which a Shakespeare emerges. Language, like soil, grows flourishing plants out of its extravagance, a munificent queen who tosses up her wealth in wild greenery to all comers. One well might fear the machine-language and machine-society we have already nearly created, were it not for precisely this extravagance, which brooks no constraint and bursts forth in unexpected bright colors even from the pavement. Even in so-called outer space, however far we might fly from earth, irrepressible people will still create new languages, new words, new slang, for shining metal and whirring gears are no obstacle to the ceaseless creativity of everyday speech.

How callous we are toward the soil! It is open to everything we pour upon it, and when you hold it up to the sun, you can see that between its glittering facets are spaces, the spaces that accept everything without complaint. Into them roots sink, and through them plants rise. And so it is with language, for though it is the element in which we move, we take it as something solid, tangible, when in truth it is like the soil: crystalline grains and space. We take words as we take the soil, to be discrete and substantial things, entities really, when the truth is that both words and soil are like solidified sky.

Modernity makes it easy for us to ignore these immense riches of even the tiniest patch of soil, for there is nothing so leveling, so blinding as seeking profit. Driving through some fertile valleys in America, you'll see vast, perfectly flat fields—the earth made absolutely level by some great machine that balances itself with lasers like a tightrope walker's pole. Such fields could as well be indoors, or on some space station far from earth: the soil is but a machine part, the thing that is leveled. Thoreau once raged against a German scientist's nightmarish vision of just such a machine—but now such things are taken for granted. Surely the next step is to dispense with dirt entirely, people feeding upon little pills or plastic-coated facsimile foods that they are conditioned to believe delightful, not monstrous.

And closer to home, about a half mile away in fact, a man not long ago sold the swamp behind his business for an apartment complex. Awash in federal dollars, the fly-by-night company that specialized in such fiascos appeared overnight with its bent and hunched, treaded earth-shovelers and bulldozers, its fleet of hard-hatted directors and screaming wood-chipper machines. Where once was a swamp now was ripped earth, heaps of black and twisted roots, sand, and peat together in ragged waves, torn, barked chunks of trees, and heaps of broken concrete for fill. Our society rewards such ventures—indeed, this couldn't have happened without federal and state tax money. Watching a project like this, one wonders where this callous destruction will end.

By contrast, when you farm you become indivisible from the land you farm. We eat vegetables grown in local soil, and in this way eat the earth itself; we partake of it, have communion with it. Take, eat, for this is my body: but we have forgotten substantial presence, and think that it is the same when we eat a vegetable from halfway round the world. Who knows what hidden nourishment comes from eating fruit or vegetables grown in soil cared for by generations of the same family? How, in eating such food, can we separate it from the people who have gone before, or from the earth that they have tilled and made more fruitful? Reading, we read the past; eating, we eat the past; and both are real communions.

But every locale is different. It is easy to speak of globalism, but the truth is that one region varies so from another even in adjoining counties as to be a different country. Those who farm in one kind of terrain would undoubtedly be lost in another and require a lifetime to understand its idiosyncrasies—indeed, it takes accumulated lifetimes to know one small area, and even then something new is always unveiling itself. A mere few hundred feet on our farm can mean the difference between murky swamp water or bracken and an alfalfa field, between sandy loam and clay, between a vineyard and blueberries. Thus a farm is itself a community, and your communion with it is conditioned by each member: or we could say, a farm is a body, and your communion is with every member.

In such places you cannot farm with some great grading machine; you cannot ignore the terrain, but rather must be defined by it, must live with the soil as it is. You can only help it be what it already is *in potentia*; you cannot make it something else. You cannot grow asparagus in black peat, nor could you grow blueberries on high apple ground; nor, certainly, can you grow a single vast crop on such diverse land as ours. While an industrial magnate would undoubtedly deplore the soil's lack of uniformity, the truth is that it is with the earth as it is with people: the more diverse, the richer and more beautiful. We grow peaches and sweet corn, raspberries and blueberries, a dozen varieties of apples and cherries and strawberries besides—we have raised dairy cattle and chickens, grown potatoes, grapes, and green peppers, alfalfa and tomatoes and plums. Each has its proper soil, its personality.

Some say that the powers are withdrawing from earth and water, herbs no longer bearing the mysterious medicines they once did. Our world, some claim, is growing pale and enervated. Perhaps this is so: I have reason to believe it. Still, I have a friend who extracts essences from plants and collects dew to further his plant alchemy—though there is no profit in it, he holds that his efforts bring benefits other than monetary gain. We do not have means to compare his efforts with antiquity: we live today, not in the past, and must make do with what is here now. Perhaps all farming is like my friend's plant alchemy, extracting the essence of the land by way of crops and distributing it like the host among all those who will accept it.

Every farmer, like every creator of literature, works in nature's alembic, helping bring life forth out of the soil anew each year. And none would say that this crop or that is wholly his own work, for all such labor brings forth fruit only through nature and the invisible. Who can tell us whence the artist's inspiration comes, or how a plant grows, why a blossom opens up and drinks in the sun? Not even the greatest scientist in a thousand years could explain these mysteries. These are the works of primal creation, and every man who stands in his field, everyone who has set pen to paper and written words to outlast time, everyone who has felt creation emergent without and within, has touched upon the mystery of life itself. Blessed, they know what it is to be fully human, for we are fully human only when we know this mystery, and we can never know enough of it.

# After Words

*Panta rhei.* All is flux, said Heraclitus, in an aphoristic fragment whose existence itself reflects how only shards from the past remain, sometimes in context, sometimes not. A farm is not fixed, but eminently mutable, its permanence only assigned to it by us humans, who are so enamored of concepts like ownership and boundaries that we do not always see what is right before us. We think of a place as a permanent and unchanging thing, but our very act of recalling a landscape is itself an altering and forming act: the mind's eye, seeing, alters, and we often don't notice how the landscape we knew is becoming another.

During my father's childhood, the west side of Grand Rapids was farmland and woodland; the road that runs past our farm was a dirt two-track, along which wagons trundled, pulled by stolid, thick-but-tocked plowhorses. There was a little one-room schoolhouse the next road over, a mile west, and you can still see its remains, the fragments of the building where the farmchildren in the area learned their abcedaria, coming and going, getting into fights, perhaps forming a crush on a girl or boy, walking back and forth along these very roads, and never once thinking, I fancy, that the very landscape would so utterly change during their lifetime as to be nearly unrecognizable.

Take the hill just to the west of Grand Rapids, overlooking the city from Lake Michigan Drive. That hill—high, sandy ground—

was laid out in cherry orchards, row upon row of cherry trees that now one must struggle to imagine, try to reconstruct in the mind's eye. What fields were here? Where was there a red-painted, long-planked barn, into which some grizzled man no one remembers anymore brought hay for his cattle and horses, forked out manure onto a wagon, later to be forked off, deposited at the base of his fruit trees or into his fields? Where is the farmhouse, spare but neat, where he and his wife raised children, where he died late one night, while cloud wisps passed before an Arabian full moon? Where is the lane lined by wide maples down which he took fruit to market? Do these places still exist, as the poet Rilke said, in some magical translated consciousness, stored like jewels in a memory vaster than ours?

For they do not exist in this world now. Were that farmer's wife to ride down her familiar lane a scant sixty years later, she wouldn't recognize the landscape that she had seen every day of her life. How unfamiliar it all would be, these rows of houses, each insular, neighbors in name only, the roll of hills hidden away under layers of pavement, the woods and the fruit trees long since gone, the barns vanished, and the two-track become a roaring five-lane highway. What giddy changes we have lived through and take for granted, as though we had gained the powers of magi and, like the sorceror's apprentice, had so recklessly asked for changes that we entirely forgot how things once were! But our changes are often apparati, wires and gadgets, our sorcery merely machinery and circuits, and after all is said and done, we still walk upon the earth, however changed it may seem.

Are we really conscious of just how great these changes are? In 1920, Michigan had 19 million acres of farmland; and in the twenty-year span from 1954 to 1974 alone, more than one-third of that land, 5.8 million acres, was lost from farming. This was the era of unquestioned "progress," during which golf courses and highways, apartment complexes and subdivisions appeared, all the myriad forms of "growth" and "development" that the automobile spawned. In the late twentieth century, this Michigan farmland loss continued, 133,000 square miles a year disappearing, from 1982 to 1992, amounting to ten acres an hour, every hour, day after day. But such figures are abstract, and only through knowing a specific place can their meaning be realized.

That is why I have written this book, for I have been fortunate, have had an opportunity granted to less than one percent of the American population these days: I grew up on a farm. This book is about that farm, an introduction to the tapestry of memory out of which that farm's landscape is woven for me, from which it is inseparable. But I wonder just what kind of world we are bringing about, and why. We are recklessly developing what Michigan author Russell Kirk called an "inhumane world"—or worse—and even if for only a moment, I would ask you to think about why.

How little we think about whether the changes we have made can be reversed. This farmland in western Michigan is a rare thing: high, well drained, a mixture of sandy loam and clay with rich black swamp earth—indeed, so complex a texture is it that a soil mapper would have a task more intricate than the creator of any ancient mosaic, for the soil often changes in hue and kind from one step to the next, here pale, there darker, here sandy. What must it be like for such earth—whose pleasure is in bearing fruit—to be held captive beneath an impermeable layer of pavement? Isn't this why the earth constantly sends forth sprouts, tendrils that slowly crack these carapaces we so heedlessly place over her? Who among us can create even a handful of the soil that sustains us? And who can restore fertility laid waste? We need no enemies abroad: we lay waste to and salt our own land behind us.

I have a dream: I envision teams of diligent hand laborers plowing up golf courses with mules, figuring out how to push buildings into their foundations and how to break up pavement and reveal the earth longing for air down beneath it. I imagine progress toward a way of life that does not depend on constant destruction, that does not feed on the legacy we leave to our children. I can see, in my mind's eye, parking lots being broken apart, the sand beneath removed, loads of manure being brought in, and slowly the earth being restored to its former fertility.

But many things cannot be undone, and this is why we must think about what has happened and what is happening to our land. The Jeffersonian dream for America, a land of small, stable farms, of responsible people for whom family and land and religion are all interwoven, this dream is not quite vanished, but it is increasingly rare. Instead, we see a society infatuated by mirages, by the illusory images of quick dollars and no recognition of consequences, a society now so divorced from the land that many people don't even know whence comes the food that they buy. Larger and more are the watchwords by which people now live, and increasingly the world is ruled by vast commercial empires beholden to no one and nothing but their own monetary aggrandizement.

Ah, but, you say, how could our present society exist, were it not for our infatuation with the new, with the bigger, and most of all, with death and destruction, whatever euphemism we might employ? I confess I don't know. I suppose we'd have to have a new society, and an actual culture, one grounded in love of one's native place, of one's community, and of the divine. But I'll desist in arguing, for I've found it mostly evaporates anyway, and that what matters is the earth, out of which we always get our sustenance in the end. What's more, the time may come when we find ourselves perforce engaging in reverse development, the undoing of almost all our feverish doing, even a kind of judgment day.

Yet I do not call for such a reckoning—that will come on its own, whether we like it or not—but only for a recognition of what has been and is important in our lives, those of us who have grown up on a true family farm and who want it to continue. It is surely not so much to ask for: a simple acknowledgment that what has been most important to humanity for its entire existence—spirituality, family, fertile land—be allowed to survive. Already we are oddities, against whom a thousand forces seem arrayed; and this little island farm has only fragile bulwarks against a world bent on its own immolation, aflame with desire for acquisition at any cost. If you look, you can see the final battle writ small now, reflected in little decisions: to sell or to preserve this piece of land, to insist on multinationalism or to affirm the local, the immediate. This is the battle to preserve or to destroy what truly matters, what is dear. Every day is judgment day.

But this book is about people and land, specific people and specific land, about my great-grandparents and grandparents and parents and uncles and aunts, my cousins and siblings and all those who have worked on our land. It is about the land itself, about its trees and animals, about the way the sky looks on a sunny late autumn day, when the light hits everything slant and golden, about what it means to work, and about friendship and all the countless ways we are each joined to each, joined to the land and wind and rain, to the snow and to one another on a place that itself changes, is transformed with time and circumstance, and for which in the end the only continuity comes from mutual caring. It is a story of love.

The farm is what remains after words—or will only words remain?